Round About Close to Midnight

40p

Also by Mike Zwerin (Quartet Books)

Close Enough for Jazz (autobiography)
La Tristesse de Saint Louis: Swing under the Nazis

ROUND ABOUT
CLOSE TO MIDNIGHT

The Jazz Writings of Boris Vian

Translated and edited by
Mike Zwerin

Quartet Books
London   New York

First published in English by Quartet Books Limited 1988
A member of the Namara Group
27/29 Goodge Street, London W1P 1FD

Translation copyright © Mike Zwerin 1988

Originally published by Christian Bourgois as *Ecrits sur le jazz* (2 vols.)

British Library Cataloguing in Publication Data

Vian, Boris
    Round about close to midnight: the jazz writings of
    Boris Vian.
    1. Jazz
    I. Title   II. Zwerin, Michael, 1930–
    III. Ecrits sur le jazz. English
    785.42

    ISBN 0-7043-2619-1

Typeset by MC Typeset Ltd, Chatham, Kent
Printed and bound in Great Britain at
The Camelot Press Ltd, Southampton

CONTENTS

INTRODUCTION

by Miles Kington

I have always thought that Boris Vian was one of the top half-dozen jazz writers of all time, and I think Mike Zwerin is another, so I sat down to write this introduction with considerable pleasure and envy. It has to be said at once that the standard of jazz writing has never been high, as writers have always thought it more important to get across their prejudices or list their credentials than to entrance the audience with anything approaching style. American writers have usually tended to approach jazz as if it were either a branch of showbiz or a subject for a college thesis; British writers have often treated jazz as if it were another kind of train-spotting and became obsessed with dates, personnels and record numbers. Most of the famous French jazz critics have used jazz as a battleground whereon to attempt murder of other critics with whom they disagreed. That is why they were famous, rather than because anyone abroad had read them.

But now and again, while thumbing through jazz writing, you get that authentic thrill which you get from jazz itself, when you recognize the spark and excitement of an individual voice that knows what it is doing and does it supremely well. I get it today from Zwerin, who is an American living in France, and I got it from Boris Vian, who in some ways was an American living in a

French skin; both of them, at any rate, managed to escape the national way of thinking and to become original writers. When you are writing about jazz, a love of writing is just as important as a love of jazz and not slightly suspect, as British jazz lovers used to think – still do, most of them.

In the ten years in which he flourished after the war, one of Vian's functions was to do a monthly report on jazz publications in other countries, and as this is a side of him which Zwerin hasn't had space to include, here's a brief extract from a September 1949 round-up.

I find *Jazz Journal*, the English magazine, fairly hard to sum up neatly as everything there is written by regular columnists. But at least there is a new columnist this month, and a woman to boot (I feel the blood quicken within me) called Joan Snarey, who has written 'Jazz: A Female Point of View'. Well, I hope that Joan is blessed with terrific good looks, because if she is not she is going to have a hard passage through life. We are sometimes told, are we not, gentlemen, that English jazz fans are narrow-minded (I have often told you so myself, come to think of it) but until we meet female English jazz fans we do not know what real narrow-mindedness is. Learn then, fair French readerettes, that according to Miss Snarey any group which contains a saxophone (be it a soprano played by Bechet or a tenor played by Hawk) cannot hope to be recognized as a real jazz group. When you are as in love with the past as Joan is, you must derive total ecstasy from records like those of the Gramercy Five on which Johnny Guarnieri plays harpsichord. To judge a musician not by the way he plays but by the instrument he plays is a revolutionary new approach for a critic, and I think it has a lot to recommend it; so let us pay due tribute to an Englishwoman for having discovered it . . . Ah, Françoise, where have you been all this time? Why don't you write to me any more? Send me a photo! Give me a rendezvous! I'm so miserable without you . . . But I digress. Joan, by the way, also loves the late Bunk Johnson. I'm not surprised. She loves all things dead. Luckily, if I want a fairer idea of the place of women in British jazz, I can get it from Kathleen Stobart. To sum up, *Jazz Journal* may have contained good things this month, but I felt too ill to read on.

Good, light-footed stuff, in which Vian uses humour to knock down a prejudice instead of the usual anger or earnestness. What British critic would have bothered to read a French jazz publication in 1949? Or in 1988, come to that? And which British writer would have the temerity to include a passionate aside to his missing girlfriend as a throwaway gag? And the fact that Vian should have spotted the talent of Kathy Stobart, who is playing as well as ever here in 1988, gives his work a sudden modern tinge. Substitute synthesizer for saxophone and you get another modern tinge.

Vian had all the credentials to be a good jazz writer. He was a good enough trumpeter to play professionally, he wrote hundreds of songs and is on record singing some of them, and he knew English well enough to talk to all the musicians – well enough, indeed, to be the French translator of Chandler's novels, Algren's *The Man with the Golden Arm* and Brendan Behan's *The Quare Fellow*. He wrote five novels, of which two (*L'Automne à Pekin* and *L'Ecume des jours*) are near-masterpieces, and he also, as a joke, wrote a sadistic and erotic thriller under an American pseudonym which took him a fortnight to write and became a runaway best-seller in 1946. Actually, he suffered from this in some ways, as his authorship of *I Shall Spit on Your Graves* by Vernon Sullivan became the most famous thing about him, and the one that obituarists most remembered when he died in 1959.

He gave up writing novels in the 1950s. He gave up playing the trumpet because he had a bad heart. But his passion for jazz continued right to his early death (he was thirty-nine) and it is that passion which turned all his other qualities into something remarkable. It was a time of strife in jazz, the ancients *v.* the moderns, a time when the Hot Club de France could expel the Strasbourg branch in 1956 for having the temerity to arrange a concert by Chet Baker, but Vian rises above all this petty warfare like a god in a balloon, dropping bombs and bouquets on both sides, and leaving behind an exhilarating collection of eye-witness reports. In a way, the 1950s were the most exciting decade jazz has ever known. *Wire* magazine recently asked its youthful writers to name their 100 most important jazz LPs, and if it came as a shock to find the magazine specifying that nothing pre-1940 was to be voted for, it was even more of a shock to find that the 1950s and 1960s came out in that voting as more interesting by far than the 1970s or 1980s.

The 1950s were certainly the last decade before rock 'n' roll trampled all before it, dulling the eardrums and clouding the airwaves. Reading Vian, I get an image of clear skies and bright, sharp landscapes, before the air became polluted by noise and drum-machines. Not by reading one piece, perhaps, which isn't enough to get you into his world. But read ten, and you start to relax. Read twenty, and you get carried away by his passion, his knockabout and/or subtle humour, his literary verve, his sheer joy in the music and all who love it – and by the ever-present feeling that there is something totally ridiculous about being a jazz critic when you could be listening to or playing the music.

Incidentally, Vian reports in 1949 that rumours reach him of some great new records by Miles Davis, though he doesn't know the personnel. These are the records later to be dubbed 'The Birth of the Cool'; they are also the records on which Mike Zwerin might have played, if fate had been kinder, as he relates in his own book *Close Enough for Jazz*. It's the only near-link between the two that I know of – until now, that is, when Mike's prose turned out to be the right channel to get Vian into English. I think Boris would have approved.

TRANSLATOR'S PREFACE

Before starting to translate his jazz writing, I thought Boris Vian was the best jazz writer of all time. Since finishing, I'm sure of it.

Translating Vian has made me a better jazz writer. He taught me how to approach a 'serious' subject with humour, and how to be seriously humorous. Jazz musicians would benefit from reading Vian. He integrated the physical and the intellectual, the real and the surreal, and he swings with words the way a jazz player ought to swing with notes.

He hits the occasional clinker (who doesn't?) With hindsight, he can be called sexist, and Crow Jim. He was a product of his times. His foresight, however, could be astonishing. He predicted post-bebop ('free jazz') collective improvisation. His arguments in favour of Charlie Parker and Dizzy Gillespie – for an acceptance of the organic evolution of jazz – could have been written in the eighties substituting the name Miles Davis.

The impact of Vian's syntax on contemporary French writing might be compared to Kerouac, or even Hemingway. Hip post-May, '68 French prose, the incorporation of street rhythms and argot into 'serious' writing, is a product of Vian – as illustrated by the influential daily newspaper *Libération* and the mass-circulation monthly *Actuel*. I hope this translation helps produce a similar effect on the syntax of English-language jazz criticism.

Having to write fast for deadlines and low prices, he made the occasional factual errors (I have corrected them), and for the same reason he repeated licks (who doesn't?), though usually for different audiences (a jazz magazine and a daily newspaper) and in other contexts. I have eliminated outright redundancies.

As with most journalists, editorial policy took away his titling rights (journalists rarely get the final cut), and newspaper and magazine editors tend to be, shall we say, unimaginative. I changed some heads to something closer to Vian's style.

'My shit is not translatable,' I kept hearing him whisper into my mind's ear, as he laughed at me from wherever he may be, I fondly hope, laughing in peace. Remembering Yevgeny Yevtushenko's (sexist) remark that: 'Translation is like a woman. If it's beautiful it's not faithful; if it's faithful it's not beautiful,' I tried to put myself into Vian's skin and adapt his loose, colloquial and yet Cartesian French into an English prose style he would have written if he had written in English. I can already hear the critical wail: 'What presumption!'

You bet, Hugusse. Presume!

I turned his puns on the names of French critics and musicians into puns on the names of Anglo-Americans. Vian enjoyed calling Hugues ('Hugusse') Panassié 'Pain-acier', literally 'Bread-steel'. I translated this not-so-playful disrespect into 'Pain-ass-ié', which I bet my bottom franc (no bet-hedger I) he would approve of. 'Zoiseau' (for Charlie Parker) became 'Ze Bird'. He illustrates the prototype nowhere with the name of a French town in the middle of nowhere, Grives-le-Gaillard, which means nothing to Anglo-American readers – I made it Oshkosh. So on.

Pieces with only French relevance were dropped, as were those which have failed the test of time. I am not a great believer in releasing every out-take by Ze Bird.

It is interesting to note how Vian's 'chops' improve over the years. As he gets more familiar with the 'tunes', his interpretation becomes richer and more convincing. He appears to have felt most at home writing for *Jazz News*, of which he was also the editor-in-chief. He wrote more than one article an issue, behind a 'nom de guerre' like Andy Blackchic, Michel Delaroche and Dr Freddy Flabby.

The order of the collection is basically chronological.

However, like any professional journalist, Vian's creative bursts came between episodes of (cringe) 'serious' journalism. And the energy level of his jazz writing would obviously have gone down when he was working on a novel. I shuffled some of the heavyweight pieces out of time to jolt the reader just when it might seem that Vian was getting too, well, you know ... professional.

Sufficeth to say (sufficeth??!!) that translating the title story, the 'Letter to Santa Klaus' and 'Papal Decrees' were nightmares – though for some reason I could always understand, I kept waking up laughing.

Jazzistically bizarroid.

MIKE ZWERIN, January 1988, Paris

Thanks to: Annie Amirda, Maurice Girodias, Bernard Giquel, Bernard Loupias, Francoise Pasteau and Benjamin and Martine Zwerin

ROUND ABOUT CLOSE TO MIDNIGHT

A Fairly Fairy Tale

'Yodel . . . yodel . . . yodel . . . yodel . . .'
(Gillespie, *Collected Works*)

'What is this bipop?'
(Paul Boubal, *Poetic Anthology*)

(*Jazz Hot*: Christmas, 1948)

The doorbell rang like a fast Brownian lick. I listened more carefully. There was no doubt. Somebody was imitating the trumpet solo on Ray Brown's 'One Bass Hit'.

Sluggish with sleep, I got out of bed, slipped into my pants and a sweater and went to open the door. Who could it be at this hour? I tried to get my head together. Maybe a policeman had come to arrest me for outraging public decency under the covers of jazz magazines.

I opened the door. A man walked right in. He was small and shrivelled, about fifty years old at first sight. He looked familiar except for his bulging stomach. He raised his right arm in the Nazi salute: 'Heil Gillespie!'

He clicked his heels twice up-tempo like those two brass chords in 'Stay on It'. ('That must be hard to do,' I muttered to nobody in particular.)

1

'Heil Parker!' I responded automatically.

'Permit me to introduce myself,' he said. 'Goebbels – special propaganda delegate to the UN Musical Commission, Jazzband Department.'

'Goebbels?' The name was familiar. I searched my memory. 'You used to be thinner,' I said finally. 'Didn't they hang you?'

'And Ilse Koch?' he asked with a big smile. 'Did they hang her too?'

'What? . . .'

'I did the same thing she did,' he said, lowering his head, blushing. 'I got pregnant in prison. The Americans freed me. I get along rather well with Americans, especially after they heard my "Flight of the Bumblebee Rag" played by the Moscow Railroadman Jazz Band. When they needed a bebropagandist, I was the obvious choice.'

'And Goering?' I asked. 'What about Goering? Is he obviously anything?'

'He plays bongos in the UN bop combo.'

We were still standing in my vestibule. 'Come in,' I said. 'We obviously have important Things to Come together.'

*   *   *

He lifted a glass of elixir of cannibis and toasted: 'To our beloved Birdland.' After eating a small opium cookie, he continued: 'I'll explain why I've come for your help.'

'But I'm not qualified to help you,' I said.

'On the contrary,' Goebbels answered, 'nobody takes you seriously. That's Handy. It's a perfect cover. We must be prepared to spy for Herr Gillespie!'

He got up and clicked his heels like those two chords again: 'All for bebop!' he exclaimed, sitting back down. 'And now let's talk Buzzyness. Look at this, you will see how others have set an example . . .'

He handed me a piece of paper. It was a tract signed by the French Plumbers Union. It read: 'The union requests all its members, as of January 1st, 1949, to replace brass and steel screws with Zincleton. Vive Zutty! Long live Plumbers! Vive Mezzrow! Vive le Republic-o-reeny! Smrt fasizmu! Svoboda narodu.'

2

'But this is Sabbytage!' I exclaimed, Furioso. I should have known it.

'Just camouflage, baby,' Goebbels said. 'And did you Getz the code at the end?'

'No. What's it all about?'

He laughed. (Bop.)* 'You'll see. Let's cut out and scarf some frim-fram sauce.'

*   *   *

We sat down in a Chinese restaurant. 'The do-re-mi of bebropaganda,' he began, 'is to infiltrate the language with our own jive. Dig!'

He called the waiter and ordered wild Reece with Steamin' pea-bop soup. Getting the idea, I asked for a pot of Tea-lonious. The waiter almost fainted. Goebbels pointed to him and shook my hand with a Spring of Joy: 'That cat will remember this night for the rest of his life. Get the Groove, Holmes?'

'It seems obvious,' I said.

'Maybe for you,' replied Goebbels. 'You've already Serged Miles Ahead. But for them, the squares, the straight studs . . . do you realize the Richies and Powell we can have?'

The waiter was writhing in agony on the floor. He did not seem well at all. I Lewist my appetite.

'Let's go someplace else,' I suggested. 'How about the Bolling alley in Phil Woods?'

'Fine. But first a bottle of Dexter Corton, 1942.'

'I think I'd prefer soda-bop,' I said. 'I'm not feeling Wallington enough to go bar-bopping. I'd Rodney Stitt down for a while. Anyway we're getting Carneyd away. Let's try and be reasonnyble.'

'No. The more unreasonnyble the better,' he replied. We went outside: 'You don't have a Basie understanding of propaganda. Aren't there people who have never understood one word in any article ever written by André Hodeir? Of course there are. But Hodeir writes books about jazz, they're published by Larousse, a very serious company. And people who read his

---

(*Editor's note)

books generally consider him one of the best jazz critics. That's only one example.'

'Zoot alors!' I exclaimed.

'There's no shortage of ideas in the UN Musical Commission, Jazzband Department. We plan to publish a book about Urbie Greenbelts entitled "Megabopoli". Colonel Tom Parker is changing his name to Charlie. Jimmy Carter, a young politician in Georgia, will change his to Ron. Through our sophisticated long-term infiltration techniques, we are grooming Charlie's piano player Al Haig for Secretary of State. Dizzy Gillespie has decided to run for president so he can sing "Salt Peanuts" in the White House. Now's the Time to get going before it Petersons out.'

*   *   *

Approaching Boulevard Saint-Germain, we Passed a bookstore.

'Let's go in here,' said Goebbels.

'I would like the complete works of Leon B. Bopp,' he said to the clerk.

'I'm sorry, we don't stock that,' the clerk replied, puffing on a musicians' cigarette. 'But may I suggest "Vian with the Wind" by George Mitchell instead?'

'No,' said Goebbels, 'and don't Purdie me on.'

We left Pretty fast.

'Did you see him bebogarting that Roach?' Goebbels axed. 'He's counter-revolutionary. We must brainMarsh him to the Max.'

'Don't fight windmills,' I advised. 'Let's not make enemies in Groovin' High places. I get along quite well with the Archiedemie Française and they have agreed to replace the syllable "van" by my name. It won't cost them much, and I need the publicity. We both need the publicity.'

'That's not the problem,' he replied, worried. 'That book was written by *Blue* Mitchell, not George. Wait! Who's that Duking out the door?'

I recognized the bookseller. He was in a Rushing.

'Wow!' said Goebbels. 'He's Something Else. He's Flyin' Home. We've got to find out what's Hamptoning.'

'What if we take a Shorty cut?' I proposed. 'It might be

Tough, but . . .'

'Shorty?! White West Coast Shorty *Rogers*?' Goebbels looked at me, paling with anger. 'And did I hear you say Tough? *Dave* Tough? Rhymes with Stuff? Another chalk-faced impostor.'

I turned white with fear – Whitey Mitchell white . . . whiter, white as Stan Kenton. 'Dave Tough's not all that Whiteman,' I said.

Goebbels reached into the pocket of his Black, Brown and Beige jacket. He pulled a metal object far-out and then there was a loud 'CLICK!'

*   *   *

The receiver clicked as I picked it up. The phone must have been ringing for five minutes. I came out of my round-Midnightmare and mumbled: 'HiLow. Sleepy John Estes here.'

'Hello,' I heard. 'It's Hodeir . . . Hello?'

'Hodeir? Which Hodeir? The Hodeir that rhymes with Brubeck?'

'What's wrong with you? It's André. Did you Wright your editorial for the Christmas issue?'

'No. You'd better do it this year,' I sighed, awake by now. 'My Dickie doesn't feel very Wells. I can't Garner enough strength.'

'Come on,' Hodeir laughed. 'It's too late for you and me to change Erroles.

First Time Since Before the War

(*Combat*: 5 December, 1946)

Nineteen-thirty-nine was doubly-triste for jazz fans. In the first place there was the catastrophe nobody needs to be reminded about, and then it caused Jimmie Lunceford to cancel his scheduled concerts here. The world has apparently not yet recovered from the former, but we seem to be getting consolation for the latter – Don Redman's band is in Paris.

The Taxi's on Fire

One telephone call and three contradictory cables washed up in the Hot Club office yesterday morning. That flood of communication left one important question unanswered: was Don Redman coming or not? In the end the answer was no, it was unavoidable but still annoying. In any case everything was finally settled and this afternoon a reduced formation (thirteen musicians) recorded six sides for the Swing label.

Great excitement was created by the presence of such exuberant individuals as Don Byas, the tenorman who unseated Coleman Hawkins for the first time in the most recent *Esquire*

6

poll; Billy Taylor, a pianist to smack our lips over; Buford
Oliver, a fine and elegant drummer; Tyree Glenn, built like
Tarzan with shining fawn-coloured eyes and wearing a sensational necktie; Peanuts Holland, a small unpretentious always
smiling man, and bassist Ted Sturgis, who was late because of
an unforeseen accident. A taxi commandeered in great haste for
the two of them by Hubert Rostaing caught fire just-like-that
three kilometres before arriving at the session. It might as well
have been twenty-five. They played only on the final side.

Marijuana, a Saxophonist and Bicarbonate of Soda

I could not go to the recording session. I hear it went very well
without me although I'm a little dubious of the report I received
from Pierre Artis who, it seems, had smoked a marijuana
cigarette out of curiosity and discovered that Sturgis plays better
when you're high.

'Don Byas is a master,' he also told me.

That I already knew. Byas's recordings had convinced me
of it.

I met the musicians over a few bottles after the date, at the
Hot Club de France. Here too you noticed Byas before anyone
else. He drank a glass of bicarbonate. Was he on the wagon? No.
His face was too lit up. More likely he just knew when to stop.

Byas looked at the drawings Charles Delaunay had done in
the States and slapped his leg, laughing, recognizing portraits of
his friends.

I asked the general ritual question: 'Are you happy to be in
Europe?'

'Fine,' Oliver replied, with a sly smile.

They had arrived via Denmark, Sweden and Norway. Behind
me, Peanuts Holland studied the map of the French Hot Club
regional offices with interest. I explained about the large pins
with the red heads, and he was really happy to learn that the
prettiest, which had white trim, was precisely where we were.

The Swedes Grow Grapes

Really, these guys put out relaxed and jolly vibrations you'd never find in the company of 'serious' musicians. All of them laugh all the time and they all have little trimmed moustaches and Dizzy Gillespie goatees. Impresario Timmie Rosenkranz is a big blond, but his wife Inez Cavanaugh, with her dazzling smile and mischievous ebony face, looked really fine in her astrakhan with a dark madras hood and spike-heeled shoes.

I figured she ought to be able to tell me which one is the band's 'bad boy'.

'There isn't any,' she said. But she couldn't help laughing. 'It's Buford Oliver,' she finally confessed.

Oliver's left ankle was wrapped in a big bandage and the foot was in a slipper. He was casually leaning on a cane.

'He mistook a window for a door in Sweden,' she explained.

'The Swedes must have started growing grapes,' I guessed.

'Actually he was lucky to have only one broken ankle not two,' she said. 'It was the second floor.'

I was worried. I asked for details. I can reassure you – you'll get to hear him. Because (this is confidential) it seems they want to stay here for a while.

To conclude, a piece of advice – don't miss Redman if you have come to love jazz despite all of it you don't hear on Radio France.

A Chorus for the Last Judgement

(*Jazz Hot*: December, 1946)

The Editor-in-Chief of *Jazz Hot* magazine excuses himself to his readers with regard to the mixture of person and tense and the bizarre narrative twists of this article. The truth of the matter is that the day after the interviews were conducted, we found two individuals in an advanced state of inebriation on the floor of the Hot Club offices. They were so far gone that it was a while before we recognized Ténot (Frank) and Vian (Boris). The article in question was in the inside right pocket of the former and, as the deadline was pressing, it was sent without checking to the printer. That explains this.

This big hulk galloped ahead of us as we turned the corner on to rue Chaptal.

'It's Molinetti!' Ténot exclaimed.

'No it's not. It's Fabre!'

'Molinetti!'

I started to object again when a human meteor almost tore my nose off before disappearing down the street and into the Hot Club of France office.

'And who was he?' said Ténot. '*That's* Fabre!'

9

Yes, it was true. I blushed. The first one had not been Fabre. This one was Fabre.

Ténot went in first and then another joker flew by me, shouting an imitation of screeching tyres as he braked.

'Jeezus!' Ténot exclaimed.

I exclaimed 'Jeezus!' too. *This* was Molinetti.

It was getting too complicated. We decided not to pay any more attention to it. Molinetti was wearing a beautiful necktie. He said that one of his friends had brought it from America. It was dark blue, with hand-made orange drawings of a cymbal, a saxophone and a conductor's arm holding a baton.

'It's the latest style over there,' Molinetti said. He had reason to be proud of his tie. We ushered him up the wide and brightly-lit Hot Club staircase.

Both Ténot and I were a bit, shall we say, shaky. We pushed the door open. Mon Dieu! Charles Delaunay's office was as packed as a rush-hour metro. Everybody was there, talking at once. Suddenly stumbling upon such verbal and physical animation shook us up even more.

A musician sitting in the corner kept staring at the floor as if hypnotized. Just shy probably. It was clear from the hunch of his back that he was a bass player. Vian nudged me and pointed to the dead-giveaway calluses on his fingertips. I decided to trust my journalistic instincts and moved in.

'What do you think about jazz?' I asked him.

'Me? Oh. Nuttin much.'

'What do you mean, "nothing"?'

'I don't give a shit about jazz.'

'But you're obviously a bass player. To play the bass for a living, you've got to be absolutely enthralled by jazz.'

Vian cringed when he heard 'enthralled'. Too intellectual for him.

'My "living"? Fuck! I'm a plumber. Excuse me, gov'nor, but I'm looking for a drainpipe.'

'Of course,' I said, 'anybody can see that. You better look somewhere else.'

Bizarre. Now what about youngblood over there? Obviously an apprentice bebopper passionately in love with Gillespie. But something was weird. It was too obvious. I no longer trusted my instinct. Let Vian have this hustle.

10

'Hello Cicurel,' Vian said.

It was Cicurel! A real musician after all. I'd blown it again. I kept quiet.

With his curly blond hair, Cicurel was an imposing figure. He also had a head under it: 'Bebop is anti-romantic,' he said. 'A punch in the professor's gut. An attempt to make cerebral music.'

I was confused. Don't most professors *like* cerebral music? And how did Cicurel know the answer? Vian had not even asked a question. I shook my head and cleaned my ear as Vian continued: 'And do you approve of that?'

Cicurel continued: 'There's something in that music you don't find in Armstrong. But modern music tends to drown out individual personality. You shouldn't forget that Gillespie isn't exactly typical. It's basically only "style", and when the means becomes the end, inspiration goes out the door.'

Sitting nearby, Diéval was listening.

Ferreri arrived, grumbling: 'They're Cubists.' He went out the way he came in.

'I'm in favour of maximal economy,' said Cicurel. 'If you need twenty-five notes, I might accept twenty-seven. Nobody's perfect. But never fifty.'

Diéval's glasses flashed like red lights; the rest of him was obscured by puffs of pipe smoke: 'It's excellent, professional music made by people who have studied their theory and harmony. When Ravel wrote "Jeux d'Eau", everybody said, "He's throwing everything into the garbage can," and most of the players thought they were playing wrong notes. It's the same thing with bebop right now.'

Diéval and Cicurel had Vian in a corner. He was too busy ducking to take notes. Luckily I happened to have pen and paper. I scribbled discreetly . . .

'You get the impression that they're totally outside the limits of traditional harmony,' said Diéval, 'while really they're merely stretching the limits. Instead of resolving chords the way you expect, they go through . . .???' (I didn't get what he said next. It sounded like 'Orléans', but it couldn't have been that now, could it?) '. . . inverting the chords so you can't analyse anything you hear any more. In a couple of years there will be big bands with incredible arrangements, as complex as symphonic

11

compositions. Parallel to all that, a sort of jazz chamber music will be born, like string quartets. And then there will be collective improvisation with three, four or five crack players. This is all very healthy and proves that jazz has more to it than just the idea of a "jazz band". We're talking about high-class art. And we can still listen to recordings from 1927 or '28. Just as we still listen with great pleasure to Gregorian chants, which are the roots of our modern music.'

'We shouldn't depend on technical gimmicks for originality,' Cicurel disagreed. 'Music should be expressive. Analysing chord changes won't make anything beautiful. Only a musician expressing his own personality can do that.'

I thought I heard somebody say something about Camembert.

'Look out, it's going to be bloody,' Ténot said. 'Cicurel and Diéval are about to get physical.' I noticed that Ténot's face was turning green.

Diéval said: 'Personally, I like Roquefort and not Camembert and it's none of your business.'

I wondered what all of this had to do with the price of beans. Ténot seemed to be losing control. I wiped his forehead with a pair of silk panties I'd smuggled out of the Hot Club discotheque and he began to calm down.

Ferreri passed between Cicurel and Diéval. 'They're Cubists,' he said.

Diéval puffed his pipe silently as Cicurel started a monologue which was fortunately short because he didn't have much to say.

I said hello to Charles Hary, whose blond moustache reminded me of Maria Chapdelaine . . . but that's another story, let's forget it. My love life is irrelevant. This was serious business.

'One interesting new element,' said Charles Hary. 'The rhythm section is beginning to have a melodic function.'

Cicurel said: 'Gillespie plays the tunes better than he improvises on them. Those guys are often stronger when they play in unison, when individuality becomes secondary to the collective.'

That idea about melodic rhythm sections seemed to fascinate Abadie's bassist, Zozo. I scribbled as he said to Vian: 'The rhythm section had its robot period with Cozy Cole. They had to add some sentiment.'

12

'It's wonderful,' Jourdan added. 'Sidney Catlett more than anybody. I just love it.'

Wearing a beautiful yellow scarf, Fabre said: 'I have a lot of admiration for Gillespie. He's ahead of his time. Charlie Parker even more so. That's the path to follow. You need more and more technique . . .'

Ferreri returned and said to Fabre: 'It begins and then it goes away. I don't know what any of it means. What a beautiful yellow scarf!'

They all surrounded Chaillot, who was crying like a baby: 'This cellist I heard one day in a brasserie . . .' Tears streamed down his cheeks: 'What a lovely pastoral vibrato.' I tried to calm him down, but his melancholy was contagious and I started crying too.

After we'd succeeded in calming Chaillot, he said: 'I don't like it. Music is not a physical exercise programme. Spontaneity seems to have vanished. In the old days, mediocre musicians who practised enough could eventually play something reasonable. But the French personality is too individualistic to do justice to something like bebop which requires so much regimentation. Anyway that stuff doesn't interest me.' He wiped away another tear: 'It's too tense. I like pastoral music.'

I just had time to keep him from swooning to the floor. I noticed that Frank Ténot was barely vertical himself.

Chaillot continued: 'And as far as the rhythm section is concerned, there's no more liberty at all. They're mechanics. No more vitality. No more swing.'

'What are you saying?' Molinetti objected, on the floor, trying to extricate himself from between the legs of a big guy who smiled continually and whose name nobody knew. '"No more swing"? Well there's never been so much swing in the history of jazz!'

'No. I'm telling you, no more swing,' Chaillot said. 'They're robots. Just like you.'

Molinetti got red in the face: 'A robot? Me? When I want to go "bang" I go "bang".' He broke the window of Delaunay's office gesturing wildly with his arms.

The plumber came back, freaking out because he hadn't found one drainpipe. Everybody agreed it was a shame he wasn't a glazier.

13

Barelli showed up with his flashy American glasses. He said: 'It's the jazz of the future. Gillespie is the best thing to come down the pike since Louis. Where does he find such chords? But it's difficult to swing under those conditions. The rhythm has to be as complex as the arrangements.'

'Not at all,' Ferreri bellowed from the other end of the room, 'they're Cubists! It's not so complex, a cube.'

'When Gillespie plays "Honeysuckle Rose",' Barelli said, 'it becomes totally transmogrified, totally new. There's the genius. I'd like to hear Armstrong with a bebop band.'

I picked up the pen again; Ténot was by now totally immobilized. He tends to lose control when Armstrong and bebop are mentioned in the same breath.

Bellest was there in a corner, with his charming wife. Too bad *he's* here, I thought, but after all he's the one I was supposed to interview.

'Right now Gillespie is all by himself,' Bellest said. 'Good young musicians will someday take what he's doing further in the right direction, and bad ones the wrong way. For me, personally, it goes too far already. I'm content with Roy Eldridge and Jonah Jones.'

Violà. Bellest was finished. He had spoken his piece quickly. I was on my way to interview his wife but stopped when Delaunay diverted my attention by tapping my head hard with a rolled-up Charlie Parker poster. He gave me the ray with his big eyes. I did not insist.

Christian Wagner had never heard a bebop record: 'This evolution is good,' he said anyway. 'There's nothing totally new in music. Basically, their astounding technique permits them to take dangerous risks. But that's also thanks to all the practising they do, more than any of us here I dare say.'

Now that seemed like an honest confession. Was he saying that French musicians were lazy?

'The boppers have amazing intensity,' Wagner went on. 'They see themselves as guardians of the sacred flame. The concentration required is murder. Sometimes there's a group feeling that you can compare to collective improvisation in New Orleans music. You can also compare it to certain research now going on in contemporary classical music. But it's not really new. You find traces of bebop in earlier people like Hodges and

Hawkins.'

Vian shook himself awake and mumbled: 'Raymond Scott too.' I stopped myself from making a scene. Vian is absolutely outrageous when it comes to talking about people nobody has ever heard of.

Young and calm, wearing a gorgeous bright white collar, Soudieux stoked his pipe: 'Evolution is a natural process in music. Certain things more or less just have to happen, and they happen. One example is the evolution of Duke Ellington's band. It went where it had to go. We ought to learn from things like that.'

Ténot seemed nervous again. I listened to Soudieux say: 'You get the music you need.'

Ferreri passed by once more. 'It's Cubism!' he said.

A big guy nobody knew took a letter out of his pocket and gave it to me. 'I am Paquinet's valet,' he said. 'He couldn't make it tonight. He's recording in the studio. He asked me to deliver this note.'

The note said: 'Improvisers have a tendency to become avant-garde, to try and go as far as Picasso . . .'

Paquinet should be introduced to Ferreri. 'Orchestration is getting more sophisticated,' the note continued. 'Big bands have begun to sound like symphonic orchestras, what with all the new colours and harmonic diversity.'

That's not bad. Paquinet has class. He couldn't come, but he took the trouble to write. You could bet that Ekyan or Fouad would not do the same thing. Neither would any of those other imbeciles. They couldn't write their way out of a paper bag. I said so to the valet.

'You ought to speak up about that,' he said.

'That's not my business,' I replied.

'Anyway, everything should be *self*-explanatory,' he said.

Combelle was out hunting. I hoped he wasn't gong to arrive with a rifle. But it was Rostaing who suddenly appeared, quiet and thoughtful: 'I prefer modern Ellington and Basie to bebop. Quiet evolution.'

Just then, Roger Fisbach, a pioneer from the heroic period, who had had nothing to say until now, went into the next room and put on a record. 'Hot House', by Gillespie. I could tell from the first few bars. It cleared the place out. We were crushed by a wave of musicians rushing towards the music.

'Every man for himself!' shouted Ferreri. 'The Cubists are coming!'

They ran out, one after the other. We stood there, stupefied. Just then a latecomer appeared at the bottom of the stairs. He was wearing a white robe, no shoes, and there were wings on his back.

'Mr Delaunay's office?' he asked, after tiptoeing upstairs.

'Over there,' said Artis, making the sign of the cross. Artis knew who it was right away. Personally I did not recognize him. Ténot neither.

'How do you do, Mr Delaunay,' said the winged man.

'Monsieur?' Delaunay regarded him in his usual cold fashion. He waited silently.

'I will explain,' the man said, pulling out a golden trumpet from the folds of his robe. He started to play it. It made a frightful noise.

'What do you think of that?' he asked. 'I'm Gabriel. The Archangel, as I'm known. That was my chorus for the Last Judgement.'

(Interviews by Frank Ténot and Boris Vian)

A Bizarroid Coincidence

(*Combat*: 23 October, 1947)

By an odd, even bizarroid coincidence, it so happens that my first column in this publication comes at the same time as certain important jazzistic events which I will try to explain to you. A perfect introduction.

Let's be precise from the start. When we say 'jazz', we do not mean that syrupy music called 'dance' with which those grotesque maniacs on Radio France systematically try to poison us against everything resembling real jazz. For the past dozen years or so, the Hot Club de France, the oldest Hot Club of all, has defended jazz on our behalf. Organization was messy at first but the HCF matured little by little, helped by the input of its president Hugues Panassié and his secretary-general, Charles Delaunay. This team functioned more or less well until 1940, when, tired after changing his mind every year, Panassié retired full-time to the village of Montauban in the provinces and Delaunay assumed the sole responsibility of upholding jazz during the Occupation. After the Liberation, everything slowly (oh so slowly!) got started again. The magazine *Jazz Hot* was published again. Which brings us to 1947.

Believing that after seven years of inertia the moment had come for him to reaffirm his royal prerogatives, Hugues de Montauban left his holy retreat and, having brainwashed certain

17

valiant regional Hot Club presidents, tried to infiltrate cells of these perfidious creatures into the head office. He attacked Delaunay under, to say the least, ludicrous and fallacious pretexts, lowering the debate to the level of personal vindictiveness. During the general assembly of 2 October, he succeeded in getting Delaunay fired from his post of secretary-general.

Now for some perspective. A few months ago, Delaunay edited a special edition of the magazine *America* called *Jazz 47*, entirely consecrated to jazz, which included: 1) A flight of fancy written by your humble servant accompanied by a surrealistic photo montage with – quel horreur! – the head of drummer Zutty Singleton superimposed on Rita Hayworth's semi-nude body; and: 2) a reproduction of a well-known painting with another figure in an advanced state of undress. Panassié cried 'scandal' and, blushing all over, covered his face with his hand, the fingers of which were spread discreetly apart. In addition, *Jazz 47* included an excellent article by Sartre which – it was only to be expected – received higher billing than that of Panassié. It was clear that the president's motives were diabolically intertwined with certain mundane considerations.

We had been worried that the above-mentioned disagreement might lead to a schism, a total collapse of all previously accomplished constructive work. Nevertheless, last Saturday the Hot Club de France gave a unanimous vote of confidence to Charles Delaunay. The vote was confirmed by certain regional HC offices which disapproved of the devious manoeuvres of Hugues the Great. The magazine *Jazz Hot* will continue to be edited by Delaunay, as always. The concerts in the Ecole Normale will be continued, as will a large number of special projects, some in the planning stage, some already being executed. This column will keep you informed of the essentials as well as peripheral amusements as they occur – so long as you keep supplying liquid refreshments.

This is the situation at the present time. A new epoch in the history of jazz is beginning, and although it may be unfortunate that two old friends are flogging each other in public, it is also certain that both of them are going to work harder because of it, which will perhaps give us the opportunity to hear a little more jazz – and to watch some spectacular Gillespian judo matches in addition.

18

To conclude this first and rather tame chronicle, I would like to give you a hint of things to come. I promise, above all, to keep you up to date with new record releases, assuming I have enough doubloons to buy them. You will also find biographical information about important jazz musicians and interviews with fantastically interesting personalities. I will assume the responsibility of letting you know about venues, places, spots and other caves where you can hear what you should hear while drinking a jug of pineapple juice. Finally I will let you in on the latest important events from faraway Amerland. I would love you to write whether you agree with me or not. If you love jazz, just remember that the more you talk about it the more it will be talked about. What we like to hear perhaps differs, but above all let's not allow our lovely music to be killed by the indifference, ignorance and impotence of blackguards, of pompous bearded moralizers or finger-waving pontificators for whom a Negro is a bootblack and a plunger-muted trumpet an invention of the horned devil. There are also lots of other people to abuse; I promise not to fail in my duty – I swear on the head of Duke Ellington.

Rutabagas and Carantines*

(*Combat*: 30 October, 1947)

The scolding of the week is aimed at that two-headed monster Columbia and His Master's Voice. The individuals who preside over the baking of our favourite round black pancakes have decided that it would be clever to couple them, twice in a short period of time, with monstrous B-sides. Three months ago, we found Glenn Miller's horror 'Falling Leaves' on the back of 'Whatta You Gonna Do?' by Louis Armstrong. And Columbia has stuck 'I Didn't Mean a Word to Say' by Harry James on to an excellent Count Basie rendition of 'Lazy Lady Blues'. It is imperative to remind these boors that the worst Armstrong is still better than the best Miller. And if I wanted to be nasty to Harry James, I would say that only this particular Harry James is revolting. Messieurs Columbia and His Master's Voice, don't try to convince me that there are not enough Basie and Armstrong masters to make two-sided discs. Your shameful policy is strangely reminiscent of those merchants who forced us to take five kilos of rutabagas for the right to buy half a can of delicious Carantines during the Occupation.

Rutabagas = swedes; *Carantines* = type of leek known to connoisseurs.

Brightany and the Kongou

(*Combat*: 6 November, 1947)

It is not too early, since it happened two weeks ago, to speak about the return of the Quintet of the Hot Club de France.

There are two reasons to mention this. First, the Quintet is a pre-war phenomenon and very few of today's young people have heard the real thing live. Then again it is our only native ensemble which can compete with American formations. Actually 'compete' is not such a good word if you see what I mean, but . . .

In short, the Quintet's music is worth listening to for those of you who have ears capable of hearing harmonious, pleasing sounds and because it is the perfect vehicle for painlessly introducing your grandparents to this primitive art we love so dearly. You can guarantee them that if they go to certain select establishments like Brightany and the Kongou they will hear something worthwhile and beautiful – and let me remind you that it is, after all, jazz, with enough improvisation to please anyone.

(*Combat*: 13 November, 1947)

Correction

In my last column, a typesetting error obscured certain lines so that the text which appeared may have led you to believe that the Quintet of the HCF is playing or has played in Brightany and the Kongou. Basically, I only wanted to advise jazz fans to buy their forebears tickets for Salle Pleyel on Sunday to hear Django & Co at home; and that you can assure them they will hear some fine music and to say that after that they can take a walk to Brightany or the Kongou for all I care.

Hugo Hackenbush and the Monkeys

(*Jazz Hot*: November, 1947)

Recently I had the curious experience of watching successive projections of *Jammin' the Blues*, Gjon Mili's famed filmed jam session with black musicians, and *Swing Romance*, a corny feature film in which Fred Astaire plays the trumpet and wins his sweetheart's hand by getting a job with Artie Shaw's band.

It was particularly interesting to observe the audience, mostly ordinary young neighbourhood people who had come primarily to see the cartoons. It was clear that they had also been looking forward to a lot of laughs during the Mili film. Think of it – a movie with nothing but Negroes clowning around making faces as they played that funny music of theirs. In short, the public was laughing before it started and they made a great effort to continue to laugh during the early moments. But other than some close-ups of the woman singer, which brought on the giggles – finally some real reason to laugh (think of it, on top of everything else, she sang in American) – it wasn't what they were expecting. 'Don't you think we have every reason to expect a few belly-laughs from people who look so much like monkeys?'

I don't think there's any need to describe the perfection of *Jammin' the Blues* still another time. You've all certainly seen it, you must still have in your mind's eye the slow twisting grey

23

cigarette smoke in front of a black background, the tranquillity with which Illinois Jacquet begins to play the blues, the flashing veneer as one saxophone and a trumpet suddenly multiply on the screen, the marvellous simplicity, the beautiful black masks sculpted in shadows by Mili's subtle lighting. I do not have to describe the two dancers redoubling an already fast tempo, or their shadows flashing on the brightly-lit backdrop, and certainly there is no need to describe this music, which is the very essence of life.

But the reaction of the audience struck me as revealing – the obligation they seemed to feel to laugh at the slightest gesture. Because these people are black, it follows that they must be clowns or monkeys.

Cut to Fred Astaire. Fred Astaire rolling his blue eyes so you could see the whites of them, Fred Astaire contorting his face, Fred Astaire twisting like a frightened spider in front of the stiff band, twirling his trumpet and aiming it towards the sky in impossible unplayable angles between turning somersaults, flapping around like a fish on a hook as he reached, or appeared to reach, clean high Fs on the instrument. Fred Astaire trying to say by his grotesque contortions: 'Look what a swinger I am,' or something like that. A sort of reincarnation of Bix Beiderbecke and Napoleon combined. Fred Astaire, his trumpet dubbed of course, unfortunately not physically dubbed as well.

And that's not all. You also see Artie Shaw and his slap-happy colleagues, from Pete Condoli to Nick Fatool. Artie Shaw, the cosmic used-car salesman . . . high, wide, handsome. No need to fabricate an image for Artie, natural charm to the tips of his toes. Mr Charm. A one-man blitzkrieg of Charm. Businessman, Lord of the Manor and even a clarinet player too. Mr Astaire and Mr Shaw remind me of Al Jolson and Ted Lewis – all those obnoxious white 'entertainers' who imitate black singers and musicians to dehumanize them, to make them appear ludicrous and grotesque – shuffling, bleating and boogying about.

But open your eyes. They are themselves the monkeys – Jolson, Lewis, even Astaire. Astaire is attractive enough so long as he sticks to his role of fashionable dancer. He only becomes unbearable when he transforms himself into something called: 'Look what a swinger I am . . .'

Now look at *Jammin' the Blues* and tell me which side, black or white, has class.

'OK, OK,' I can hear you say, 'what about Cab Calloway in *Stormy Weather*? What about him?'

Cab? He's perfect. At least he's wearing his own skin, not blackface, and we hear his own voice. And at least jazz is something basic and honest for him.

Whereas that imbecile Astaire, with his Negro costume and his silent trumpet . . . A monkey, I tell you, *that's* the monkey.

Hugo Hackenbush

WHAT'S JAZZ TO YOUTH?

(*Combat*: 29 January, 1948)

What does jazz mean to youth? Now that might sound like a silly question, as though we consider youth as a collectivity rather than a collection of individuals. But their very divergence of opinion permits the formation of a general conclusion about their reaction to this music without needing to ask if all of them agree.

For many of them jazz is only dance music, not too different from any Strauss waltz. Little do they care that there is both good and bad jazz, from Duke Ellington to Glenn Miller – it's dance music, music to flirt by, or simply choreographic gambols to advance the plots of musical comedies.

Jazz can be considered a sort of symbol of the myth of the good life which we learn about from movies – champagne, whisky, décolletage, fur coats and twenty handsome musicians playing the strains of a song the words of which our heroine whispers into the ear of her lover.

There is also the animal reaction consisting of shouting for joy as soon as they hear a drum solo, no matter how good or bad it may be. There's undoubtedly an element of snobbishness involved for some of them. During certain periods, well-meaning people have found it chic to relate to jazz, and youth followed them. Some people will follow anything.

Jazz can also be a means of protest, something to like just because your parents do not like it. Non-conformism, violence . . . Paradoxically, this is one pretext for scandal the surrealists have never explored.

Finally, there are those who are genuinely touched, first sensually, then intellectually – and in other ways like through nostalgia or to prove some theory or other – but who nevertheless are interested in looking beneath the surface, to understand, to feel, to *know*. These young people are not content to stand still, they are attracted to jazz with open minds and follow their sense of adventure to try little by little to understand the basic substance of the music.

They are the only ones who will remain faithful to jazz and follow its evolution. For the others, it will only be a passing fancy, a youthful folly, something to 'grow out of'.

LIBERTY LIGHTS OUR WAY (1)

(*Combat*: 5 November, 1948)

I understand that the United States government is preparing new laws against lynching in particular and racial discrimination in general. It is true that over the past few years the American outlook has improved concerning the thorny question of racial prejudice. Specifically, when it comes to jazz, a particularly strong effort has been made and today just homage is frequently paid to the importance of black bands.

That does not mean the question is settled. The fact that men like Ellington, Armstrong and Gillespie have by now gained status, winning polls in many American magazines, notably *Down Beat*, proves their overwhelming superiority over white bands. But we should ask ourselves if this year's poll which crowned Stan Kenton was motivated by purely musical reasons.

I can see you're sceptical. OK, here's a little story. It happened in the United States, and not even in the Deep South but in Memphis, a city which, some years ago, competed with New Orleans for the right to be called 'birthplace of the blues' and thus attract the world première of the film *Birth of the Blues*. Now however, Mr Lloyd T. Binford, president of the Memphis board of censors, has banned the film *New Orleans*, which he deemed undesirable because of a principal role played by Louis

28

Armstrong. It's an astonishing decision when you see to what point the poor Mr Armstrong is exploited in this movie.

But Mr Binford went one step further. All the scenes in which the stars King Cole, Pearl Bailey, Lena Horne etc, appear, even if only singing, have been cut. The musical comedy *Annie Get Your Gun*, which broke all records in Texas, known for its racism, was banned in Memphis because of three supporting Negro roles. Finally, *Curley*, in which black and white children play together, has also been banned.

Like hell there's no more racial prejudice in America! But does it really matter? As the critic Louis Chauvet pointed out in *Le Figaro*, Louis Armstrong probably accepted the role in *New Orleans* merely to increase his already enormous fortune.

DIZZY GILLESPIE IN PARIS

(*Combat*: 19 February, 1948)

Dizzy Gillespie's sixteen black musicians will play for the first time in France, at Salle Pleyel, tomorrow night. And so the man whom the American public has nicknamed 'King of Bebop' and who can give you, according to them, 'the thrill of your life' is finally here to thrill us.

Just about every young American jazz musician now plays bebop, a style which is, above all, the jazz played by Gillespie, Charlie Parker, Milton Jackson and a few others – just as twenties jazz can be defined by a few musicians named Oliver, Armstrong, Dodds and a few others. In fact it involves new musicians rather than new music. Despite its unnerving form, bebop is only one more inexorable step in the evolution of jazz, which was born centuries ago when the first slaves arrived from Africa in the southern United States.

The young American musicians copy everything about Dizzy, including his physical mannerisms – the beret (sometimes bright red) pulled down to ear-level, horn-rimmed glasses, moustache, goatee (a little black hairy growth on the lower lip to cushion his embouchure), and his stage manners which involve directing his band with his entire body. But they cannot copy the diabolical consistency of his attack, his confidence all over the trumpet, from the very bottom up to screech-level, his infallible harmonic instincts and the purity of his dry, clear sound – as well as the dizzying complexity of his phrases.

People who tend to think of bebop big-band arrangements as being limited unison or octave formulas are going to be surprised. Dizzy's orchestra is comprised of drummer Kenneth Clarke, whose recent recordings we have not forgotten, and nothing but young musicians. Very young. Dizzy himself is only thirty.

Just when Nice is about to give us an idea of what jazz has been, it's wonderful that Paris is presenting what it is now. We can thank Charles Delaunay who, unlike the 'technocrats' in Nice, is not subsidized. I am not forgetting what jazz owes its 'gods' like Armstrong or Hines today, but nor do I want to ignore what it will owe tomorrow to John Birks 'Dizzy' Gillespie.

(21 February, 1948)

Dizzy Gillespie and his big band played last night to a packed house in Salle Pleyel. The audience was fiery with enthusiasm.

Arriving at 8.30 p.m. at the Gare du Nord, customs chicaneries delayed the band until 9.30, forty-five minutes after the scheduled start of the concert. Jacques Danjean's trio played the thankless role of performing for an over-excited audience anxious to hear the main attraction. The curtain finally rose on the seventeen-piece formation more than two hours late.

The ambience was beyond belief. From Gillespie's first downbeat it was clear that if the majority of the audience – composed mostly of young people habituated to traditional jazz – reacted positively, there were also some who felt totally lost trying to follow the rhythm section, which had little to do with traditional forms of timekeeping. Everybody was at ease during ballads, much easier to assimilate.

Big triumph for Dizzy and his men. Only one quibble – singer Pancho Hagood, not bad though too sugary for this public waiting to be 'shocked'. On the other hand, we should mention Gillespie's remarkable use of Afro-Cuban rhythms, and his equally remarkable percussionist Chano Pozo.

Bebop, the most recent evolution in the history of jazz, has conquered Paris. Thanks to Dizzy Gillespie.

31

Liberty Lights Our Way (2)

– (A Familiar Tune)

(*Combat*: 28 March, 1948)

My most honourable faithful readers will perhaps remember my column of 5 February dealing with the harassments suffered by blacks in Memphis, and the measure taken by that fine city's head censor, Lloyd Binford, against films which feature black artists. Let us follow these exploits further. The municipality has just been ordered by an assistant to the mayor, a certain Joe Hoyle, to destroy 400 copies of three blues records described as 'obscene' by the police department of which the above-mentioned Joe Hoyle is chief.

The police chief's decision was taken, it is said, after an anonymous phone call (from a competing record company?) It appears that Boyle affirmed: 'Binford deserves a monument for having tried to clean out the movie business.' This affair assumes importance when you consider the fact that the people being purged are named Louis Armstrong, Pearl Bailey, Lena Horne etcetera.

A similar purge of Memphis radio stations is expected. But the heart of the matter is really the following – when journalists asked Boyle under what law the records were destroyed, he answered: 'The jurisdiction of the police is quite general. The law covers a multitude of sins.'

The police in other countries are also obviously on the same righteous road. Not too long ago, in fact, Paris gendarmes reacted violently to jazz fans who were pushing for autographs after Dizzy Gillespie's concert at the Salle Pleyel – they could not understand how 'civilized' people might be interested in that 'music for savages'.

The worst of it is that the good citizens of Memphis seem quite pleased with their Binford and Boyle. But if public awareness has evolved a bit further here, it is still true that at the same Gillespie concert certain spectators shouted: 'Go back to Timbuktu' and hurled the following reproach at Dizzy: 'Why don't you learn French, dirty nigger.'

I'm afraid that's the way it is.

Nice, Jazz Capital of the World: Hearing Double

(Combat: 26 February, 1948)

Every day in Nice there are two different programmes. Tonight at the opera it's Jean Leclere, Francis Burger and Mezz Mezzrow; a bit later at the casino, Louis Armstrong and Claude Luter.

Killing time before the opera concert, I polled the man on the street. After Armstrong, Baby Dodds won hands-down, probably because of his little magic number consisting of clacking two drumsticks, both held in the same hand, in a kind of tango beat, only better. I have to admit that Burger, who opened the concert, does not exactly fire me with enthusiasm. If Burger himself is not too bad a pianist, his soloists are rather annoying – they need a lot of work. As for his drummer, he could just as well not have been there.

Same thing with the drummer that followed with Leclere. I figured out why this band does not add up to all it might be. In reality it consists of two quite different half-bands – four musicians from the Bob-Shots and four Leclere regulars. Toots Thielemans, one of the latter, played 'Laura' on his harmonica and made me hunger for the astounding things he could play on a more sophisticated instrument.

34

Then it was Mezzrow's turn. Baby Dodds and James Archey were really wonderful. I was running to grab a telephone as Archey finished a triumphal 'Liza', and I leave you with the last word on tonight's concert. A stagehand at the opera cried out to the musicians: 'I hope I can play music like that when I'm as old as you are.' He was exaggerating – he was obviously already at least seventy.

Absinthe and Pastis

(*Combat*: 27 February, 1948)

There's a strong sea wind today in Nice. A good day for musicians to stay in bed. However, when I arrived at the Negresco Hotel, Lucky Thompson was already being very co-operative with a succession of interviewers. And at the bar, the inseparable Baby Dodds and James Archey. I was with some of Claude Luter's musicians, who immediately kidnapped Baby Dodds to a remote sofa where they surrounded him and asked him to clarify certain biographical details like the personnel of his bands since 1930.

Baby searched his memory for them for a good hour before, out of breath, he reached into his wallet and handed us a paper on which were written the key words: 'Absinthe and Pastis'.

'You have any?' he asked. When we told him that you can find both by the wagon-load in Nice, his joy knew no bounds. He interrupted his swooning to sign an autograph for a gentleman who kissed him on the forehead in gratitude (I did not make that up).

An embarrassing incident has, alas, just brought everybody down. A Negresco maître d'hôtel got some kicks by refusing to allow the English critic from *Melody Maker*, Max Jones, to enter the lobby, saying he was not correctly dressed. Jones, totally bald and of fragile health, is obliged to wear a beret day and night. Panassié had to use his influence to admit Jones, who asked me to teach him an appropriately vulgar French insult should something similar occur. I indignantly refused.

Armstrong, who had just woken up, crossed the lobby in kingly manner on his way to breakfast. Last night was a triumph for him, tonight will be another. You cannot really find fault with Louis. He is the same Louis you hear on record. In fact you sometimes have the impression that his records are playing, not him. Well, OK, after all, he did invent the whole thing.

Still One More Big Night

(*Combat*: 28 February, 1948)

I have not yet discussed the Derek Neville (England) or Rex Stewart (United States) orchestras in any detail. They both played Thursday night and both sounded in reasonable enough shape so that we can judge them without sounding prejudiced. Derek Neville's band is handicapped by its repertoire; all the tunes sound the same. The leader plays baritone and alto saxophones and clarinet. He overdoes the upper register of the latter two instruments, from which he squeezes the most horrible piercing sounds. I advise him to stay with the baritone, on which it is almost impossible to have that problem. That said, the soloists – Humphrey Lyttelton, trumpet; Bobby Mickleborough, trombone and Jimmy Skidmore, tenor sax – are more than honourable. I prefer Lyttelton. There is no way you could call this a bebop band.

Stewart is still the same marvellous musician we have always known. His strong personality provides the glue for a band with a split personality – Sandy Williams, trombone; Vernon Story, tenor sax and Ted Curry, drums. The latter two are much more comfortable in ultra-modern idioms than Rex and Sandy. The ensemble is not as together as it might be, but still they can satisfy even the most demanding listener.

On Friday afternoon, there was a long rehearsal in the Negresco salons to time a transatlantic radio broadcast. Claude Luter strutted about with an outsized clarinet coated with yellow wood which was at least 107 years old – a gift from one of his admirers. First Louis played and then Rex, who laughed through 'Muskrat Ramble', putting on Luter's musicians. Three minutes for one, six minutes for another; it was very complicated with eight microphones. Everybody was going crazy. On my way out I bumped into Django Reinhardt and Stéphane Grappelly, who had just arrived by train to play tomorrow as part of the 'Nuit de Nice'. I warn you in advance that I won't be able to give you a report of that event because tickets cost 5,000 francs and it's sold out.

Woodshed Your Axes

(*Combat*: 4 March, 1948)

Jazz has never been so plentiful in France as it is now, since the Great Schism which, last year, divided the two Hot Club Popes (Monseigneurs Delaunay and Panassié, to put them together despite themselves). All the faithful should find it in their hearts to bless the day this miraculous event took place.

The uproar has attracted general attention to jazz and a subsequent increasing number of concerts. For example, the city of Nice created its festival just at the right moment to compete with Gillespie as he unleashed himself on Paris.

We regret the fact that certain people take advantage of the above-mentioned Schism systematically to denigrate concerts produced by the opposing clan. They do not understand that they are, in effect, also attacking the same black musicians they profess to defend by goading them towards internal strife. The musicians, in fact, tend to agree with each other – they understand the situation well enough to see that jazz is only undergoing a normal, logical, inevitable evolution. Because one thing is certain: the definition of the word is not divided by any date, everything before being 'real jazz' and all that follows somehow phoney.

With the hope that these thinly disguised references will not

38

be taken badly by any of the interested parties (those Popes have extremely thin skin), let us proceed to another subject.

Actually, it involves the musicians themselves. Whether it be Baby Dodds (Mezz Mezzrow's drummer), Kenny Clarke (Gillespie's drummer), James Archey (Mezzrow's trombonist, one of the best-received musicians at Nice), Jack Teagarden (with Armstrong), or Gillespie's trombones – all these musicians have one thing in common: complete technical mastery of their instruments.

Today's kids play many styles – some rush headlong into bebop, others hold on desperately to tradition. But almost none of them practises. I can only assure them of one thing: whatever style they are interested in, they'll never get anywhere without learning the basics of their instruments. This might seem to be self-evident, but it's amazing how many amateurs will try to play 'Groovin' High' without even knowing that there are twelve bars in a blues.

We are fortunate to live during a time in which we have the opportunity to learn from a multitude of styles. These youngsters should take advantage of them, try and assimilate them, before jumping into a chorus which, in general, they finish, let's just say, 'with difficulty'.

THE GENE KRUPA SEXTET

**Record Review: 'Don't Take Your Love from Me';
'Imagination'; 'Coronation Hop'; 'Capital Idea';
'Paradise'; 'Overtime'.**

I'm sorry but I'm obliged to say at the beginning that I hate every
last note which splats out of Bill Harris's unspeakable instrument; and when I say that his blaring, constipated trombone
adorns almost all of the first tune, you'll understand my
reservations about it. (I was just interrupted by these guys
delivering heating oil and my hands are covered with it, which
explains the virulence of this paragraph – in oilo veritas.)

Apart from that, Ben Webster, Teddy Wilson, Ray Brown
and Charlie Shavers play admirably well on side one – there's
not much Harris on the rest of it. The slow tempos and relaxed
atmosphere on the first two tunes allow the soloists, discreetly
supported by the rhythm section, to stretch out on fine choruses
– particularly Shavers, also the arranger, who seems to be having
one of his calm, dreamy days.

The second, better side begins with a happy bright tempo,
remarkably together. Krupa's work is subtle and efficient. He's a

good team player and never gets in the way. The second and fourth tunes feature the sparkling piano of our friend Wilson. And the beautiful standard 'Paradise' is tailor-made for Shavers, who takes a lovely muted solo. Krupa lets himself loose on the fourth tune and his work is clean and swinging.

To sum up, despite that mangy Bill Harris, two very good sides. Why did they hire this lightweight who would be more at home in the pit band of the comic opera in Strudbrutch? (I'm not going to say where that is, I don't want to make anybody angry.)

THERE IS NO 'BEST'

(*Combat*: 18 March, 1948)

Jazz and jazz criticism are both in their infancy. If it is too early to write the story of the history of jazz, it is not too late to alert the public to those misguided critics who make their judgements by comparing one musician with another.

Far be it from me to lobby for criticism based on absolute values, even though I cannot deny that I fall victim to that error myself. But you have all read such phrases as: 'This one is the best tenor saxophone player since Soandso'; and: 'That one is a hundred times better than this one.' We should try and avoid this sort of judgement. This occurred to me while listening to the 1935 Red Allen recording of 'Body and Soul'.

Everybody knows Coleman Hawkins's magnificent 'Body and Soul', released in 1940, which marked, it has been said, a major step in the evolution of the jazz tenor saxophone. Critics have been falling all over each other to praise the genius of Hawkins (who is certainly inspired), and to proclaim from the rooftops that nobody has ever produced such a masterpiece. At the same time, they have been ecstatically praising this musician's ability to renew himself (it should be unnecessary to point out that at thirty-four years old, he has nothing left to prove, he has paid his dues).

42

Anyway, listen to Red Allen's 'Body and Soul'. This trumpeter never really reached the star level and, I believe, does not receive the appreciation he deserves. Comparing these two recordings is a mind-opening experience. The *spirit* of the improvisation is the same on both – each phrase tied to the next, continuity, constant searching, logical harmonic progressions. In short, identical development techniques, the only difference being inevitably due to the fact that they play two different instruments.

What can we conclude from this?

Remembering what I said at the beginning, nothing at all. What if Red Allen had himself been inspired by somebody else, less known, of whom I am unaware? What if Coleman Hawkins never heard Red's rendition?

If only I were omniscient, well, then we would have the perfect jazz critic.

News Item

Dizzy Gillespie's drummer, the phenomenal Kenny Clarke, remained in Paris when the band returned to New York. He is opening a school chez the drum manufacturer Marcel Favre in Vincennes. It appears that all the 'greats' of French drumming have already signed up. I tell you this both to plug Kenny, who is a terrific fellow, and to compliment – they are criticized often enough – the good taste of the French musicians.

KITCHEN CRITICISM

(*Jazz Hot*: September, 1952)

If you only knew how little is really going on!

Get right down to it, think hard, what do you come up with? About fifteen excellent records a year. OK, make it twenty, counting, despite my better judgement, reissues. Do you think, my generous readers, do you actually think that this miserably small output justifies the existence of fifty jazz magazines in the world?

Can't you see that everything we can print about twenty records adds up to nothing but an enormous bundle of uselessness? Because, sooner or later, you have to get back to the music itself and you are forced to say either I like this or I don't like that. And if you like it only because Whatsisname said you should like it, there's no point at all – it would be better to write about religion – Catholic or Zen, it doesn't matter, so long as the chef serves up that plate of faith which the average reader of jazzistic magazines is so hungry for.

The truth, my friends, the truth is that jazz literature should limit itself strictly to publicity – because all the explanations come a posteriori (like any self-respecting explanation) and they turn jazz into a kind of monster it was never meant to be. To try to analyse the creative process of a jazz musician in detail on the basis of what he produces is a sterile activity. Scientific analyses of a natural phenomenon, on the other hand, can change the material itself. A jazz critic will never be able to do that, even though he may know all the changes.

It has been said that jazz criticism is still too young, that it has not yet reached the perfection of Einstein's scientific criticism, which allowed him to say years in advance, in 1912, that his theories would be proved during the next solar eclipse (which they were, in 1919). Great! I wish I could do that. But take a look at another kind of more mature criticism, art criticism – everything is exactly the same as for jazz. The end result is a useless pile of undigested paper and the paintings are still in the museums.

Explain, explain! 'I don't understand,' says the viewer, standing in front of an abstract painting. But there's nothing to understand. You just have to look at it. What else can the people who 'understand' do? Very little. For them, seeing colours sets off a verbal reflex and words pour out, pour out on paper. But why this reflex? Why this? Why that? Why why or why not? It's all meaningless! I suppose we could say that people who try to share their enthusiasm can be sincere about it. And sometimes they can pull it off, but what have they gained? They have not communicated the painting, or the record, only their opinion.

That is how a lot of young people have been taken in by what Hodeir calls the 'critique d'adjectifs'. And this sort of mirage goes back a long way. It's like the story about the king who thought he was walking around in the finest clothes in the kingdom until an innocent child exclaimed, 'But the king has no clothes on!' It's an old story.

What are critics really after? I can speak only for myself, but I know what I'm looking for: to increase demand, for more opportunities to listen to Ellington, Parker, Gillespie, Louis, Ella, Peterson and the others. How to do it? Here's how. Concert promoters have fixed costs, and the fans have limited means. If the demand isn't viable for somebody, it doesn't mean anything. So? Shouldn't we try to interest the upper classes in jazz? But how? With the twenty records released every year?

Really, in all sincerity, I see only one alternative. The audience knows or doesn't know what jazz is. The critic merely helps them know a tiny little bit more. He can, however, sell it to them. So it comes down to publicity. The most hypocritical form of publicity. The propaganda is often spread by an egotistical fan who is simply more verbal than the others, who glimpses something the others don't and who wants to clarify his ideas on the subject for himself.

It's sad, after all the beautiful prose by everybody, to be so cruel about it, but it seems to me that a critic is just about as useful as a weatherman. This is how it works. There are active elements – cyclones and anti-cyclones, which is to say the musicians. They are motivated by something – a tough problem for the critic: what makes Joe Blow play? But he plays, that is the essential thing. Musicians begin to create a small audience – the first cult, which might even include a critic or two. This cult plays the role of a talent scout (is that, in fact, what a critic is?) in Hollywood. The role is analogous to an observer in the weather bureau. Specialists alert others to the fact that Joe Blow is on to something. (You can certainly call that publicity.)

Now comes the passive phase. Each one measures the reactions provoked by Blow in relation to those provoked by Jones. First on a local level and then with regard to Smith over there. They trace isobaric curves, begin to figure out that starting here, in such and such an amount of time and depending on whether this or that happens, Joe Blow will turn into this or that, he will either ravage the coast of Brittany or peter out at sea. All of which is useful information for jazz fans, and can arouse interest in jazz on the part of others who will be extremely grateful to find out if they should evacuate their houses on the coast or not. Finally Blow arrives. He either touches us or he doesn't.

What role does the critic play in all of that? Why doesn't he stay in the shadows? After all, the only thing that matters is that little map which shows us on what day at what hour the cyclone called Blow might possibly pass over Carpentras. But are we going to publish the laborious calculations of the people who spotted Blow in the first place? The public couldn't care less. The calculations interest only the calculator. What's the difference between a weatherman and a jazz critic? There isn't any, except that the weatherman doesn't pretend to be a jazz critic.

Critics do not understand that their role should be merely that

46

of a middle man, spreading news and its implications (the cyclone and its intensity). Instead they try to explain why the cyclone is what it is. To explain, always to explain. Digestion made public. They do not understand that explanations add up to nothing, they are illusions. Even the best critics do not escape this error.

The proof is that I have now been working like an asshole for an hour trying to explain why explanations serve no purpose. Anyway, I was thrilled to be so lucid today and it helped pass the time.

Should All White Jazz Musicians be Executed?

(*Combat*: 4 April, 1948)

The problem is the following: black music is increasingly encumbered by sometimes harmonious but always superfluous and usually avoidable white elements. Should we continue to congratulate and encourage the whites in question, should we criticize them or simply tell them to go take their suspenders and hang themselves?

We heard one of them, Jack Teagarden, in Armstrong's band – Teagarden's place is in the cloakroom. We saw two with Mezzrow – Mezzrow and Bob Wilber would have lost nothing but glory (and money) had they been replaced by Albert Nicholas or Bechet. We see the same problem every time there is a mixed band. Not to say that racial mixture is bad, but because in every case (example: Artie Shaw's 'Little Jazz' featuring Roy Eldridge) it would do absolutely no damage to do away with the white part of the band.

I used to be all in favour of racial integration in principle. But I have been obliged to rethink my position. Sure, it's fun to play with black musicians. But who profits from it? Surely not the blacks.

The only meaningful credential of Benny Goodman, who has

found a privileged place in the record collection of a certain number of fans (we won't bother to separate those who collect even his big-band records), is to have started the first truly multi-racial combo. All other such attempts served only to accentuate the contrast.

We are all of us too sentimental. Why accept Teagarden even though Armstrong appreciates him? Surely even Armstrong can make a mistake. For his own good, we should oblige him to hire James Archey.

But alas, the blacks are as sentimental as we are. Everybody likes to play with their friends and Teagarden is a really nice guy.

Should we bayonet all the white jazz musicians? Certainly not. But if only they'd all just drop dead . . .

ZOOT SIMS QUARTET

Record Review: 'Don't Worry About Me'; 'Crystal's'.

If we took an alto sax player and called him hubert fol (without capitals, we like to stay in vogue, mr e.e. cummings), and if we had him record two sides with gerry wiggins (piano), pierre michelot (bass) and kenny clarke (drums), it might sound like this zoot sims record. It's extraordinary at times to what extent sims's tenor sounds like an alto (especially when played at a faster speed like I'm doing). Pleasantries aside, these are two pleasant tunes. But they have the same rather annoying fault – kenny clarke's cymbals are recorded with too much treble, they grate and hum like a swarm of killer bees. zoot's a tender, confident fine little tenor player, but (it's only a quibble), those cymbals . . . Pianist gerry wiggins confirms his enormous talent. Good dance music.

REFLECTIONS ON A CONCERT BY MEZZ

(*Jazz Hot*: 22 April, 1948)

The hall was packed with enthusiastic people who were not disappointed because they had come above all to hear Mezz play his standard licks. There were no surprises that day, even though Mezz and his orchestra played better than they had recently at Nice. But then again, remember the atmosphere in the audience always plays a big part in the success of a jazz concert. Perhaps as much as the music itself.

Some words about the personnel and the performance of each.

Mezz seemed to have better chops than I remember from before the war. He's become more serious about music. But he has the unfortunate tendency to let his clarinet play all by itself, which occasionally results in too many clichés. Attractive though they may be, they are quickly forgotten.

Bob Wilber, a young curly blond student of Bechet, copies his master faithfully but he can't take off like the prodigious Sidney (this can be explained by his age and the colour of his skin, because I insist, call me 'racist' if you like, that white people will never be able to equal blacks when it comes to jazz; I'm sorry to repeat it so often but it's true nevertheless).

Harry Goodwin's trumpet playing did not fit with the style of

51

the rest of the band. It's a style I do not exactly detest – complex, influenced by Red Allen and Rex Stewart – but his sound is rough and he plays too far behind the beat to re-create the particular ambience which was so important on the recordings by Ladnier–Mezzrow–Bechet cut in 1938–9.

James Archey completed the front line and in my opinion dominated it, despite his small physical size, which can be compared to that other musical giant, Don Redman. Archey's trombone is the most exciting I've ever heard in the flesh (or the brass). Phrasing, style, imagination . . . he has it all. He has a rare quality most of his colleagues lack, or have less of: the power to make the rest of the band swing all by himself. And he's the very essence of simplicity. Long live Archey!

Sammy Price is a solid pianist, with a well-founded left hand, an excellent boogie-woogie player. In my opinion, however, he is not especially well-cast in this particular formation. This is apparently also Mezz's opinion because he had expressed his doubts to Willie Smith beforehand.

Despite his age, Pops Foster slaps the bass fiddle as it was made to be. His strength, alas, is not what it once was. But he's a pleasure to watch.

Baby Dodds, the king of New Orleans drummers, solos with a marvellous sense of humour. Baby is a unique brand of master. Flying all over the place in apparent disorder, his sticks always somehow land in exactly the right place and time.

Now the concert itself. Good grief! Everything was in it, from 'Royal Garden Blues' to 'Really the Blues', by way of any other blues you can mention. My only complaint against this sort of formula, whether it's Louis or Mezz, is that they repeat themselves. They do not replenish the repertoire with new material.

When Louis played 'You are My Lucky Star' in 1936 (was it really 1936? Never mind), it was contemporary and exciting, a real adventure. I would like to hear him continue to do the same thing. Play 'Laura' with collective improvisation, 'Laura' or anything else for that matter – anything but repeat the past repertoire note for note. And I'll tell you something. On 28 March Claude Abadie's orchestra, of which I am a member, played a series of concerts with Archey, and I spoke to Archey about my negative reactions. He said to me: 'Of course! This is the road, you want to be sure. Back home in New York, we amuse ourselves by playing "Stardust" New Orleans-style.'

But I feel – and too bad for you if you don't agree – there's no sense travelling around just imitating King Oliver. Down with fossils. I want to hear stuff I've never heard before, even if some quality or perfection is sacrificed. Actually, come to think of it, with experienced, imaginative musicians a sense of adventure does not necessarily involve loss of quality.

Heaven and Hell

(*Combat*: 27 May, 1948)

English music magazines which cover jazz (*Melody Maker* and *Musical Express*, for example) publish regular interviews with American bandleaders. As we all know, America is both paradise and hell for jazz. These interviews can furnish us with dozens of instructive examples of this. However, let's be more specific to help readers of *Combat* add to their already well-grounded education.

To this end, we will study the 16 April and 23 April issues of *Musical Express*. In the former we find an interview with Mr Kenton (Stan), in the second an interview with Mr Cole (Nat 'King'). Putting the two of them together adds up to an excellent idea for a column.

Mr Kenton leads a contemporary white band whose trumpets make more noise than Mr Jericho ever did. He is trying to 'raise the level' (his own words) of jazz. If articles by and interviews with Mr Kenton are any indication, he is a cocksure intellectual who is genuinely unhappy that jazz is perceived as vulgar, not at all intellectual music.

Journalist Bob Kreider asked him:

Q: 'Do you plan to play fewer dances and back up fewer singers in order to play more concerts?'

54

A: 'Yes. We want jazz to reach a higher level. It has now matured to the point that it can compete seriously with classical music on its own territory.'

There might, in fact, be an eventual fusion between classical music and jazz. If so, Mr Kenton is making the first step in that direction. Well now, we have plenty to talk about. I will use self-restraint and limit my comments to the remark that if this is the treatment white bandleaders have in store for jazz, it would be better – both for them and us – if they devoted their time to more serious endeavours like growing dandelions or researching the moeurs of bald giants. For Mr Kenton, no doubt, Duke Ellington works such as 'Deep South Suite' do not have enough depth to be compared with classical compositions. They will never be the equal of compositions signed Beethoven. Ellington must lack the 'Old Master Kenton touch' . . . or something like that.

An interview with Nat Cole by the same Bob Kreider appeared in the *Musical Express* of 23 April. Nat Cole is not trying to impress or win over the eleven- and twelve-year-old audience which Kenton seems determined to seduce (poor helpless innocents). Nor does Cole set himself up as the Goebbels of jazz. Among other things, Kreider asked him which of his own recordings he preferred. 'King' replied: 'It's not all over yet . . . Maybe I can tell you in a few years . . .' Then he cites people he considers to be important to contemporary music. Duke Ellington and Dizzy Gillespie of course . . . and . . . guess who. Mr Kenton (Stan).

I hope you have learned something.

STAN KENTON

Record Review: 'The Hot Canary'; 'What's New?'

'The Hot Canary' is a little, dumb, annoying number written to feature Maynard Ferguson, Stan Kenton's young 'trumpet phenomenon'. Technically speaking, a lot of people are going to be blown away – but as far as jazz is concerned Maynard should blow away somewhere himself. It has nothing to do with jazz. Why? There's absolutely no evidence of the black tradition. None – because it's in 4/4 and you can dance to it doesn't change anything. This is exactly what we call a 'novelty tune', which puts Kenton just where he ought to be – a sort of bloated Ray Ventura with less vocals, nothing else you can say for it. But let's get back to the 'Canary' in question. When we think back to Cat Anderson's chorus taking out Ellington's 'Hollywood Hangover' it's obvious that screech trumpet has a place if used correctly. ('Trumpet No End' is another example). But gratuitous screeching without any content or rationalization has nothing going for it but technique. On the other side, Ferguson earns some of our respect with beautiful ballad playing. But why

56

the double tempo, as unjustified as anything unjustifiable can be? Monsieur Kenton, you're the most tasteless American musician of all – and believe me there are a lot of them.

Typing Monkeys

(*Combat*: 10 June, 1948)

The stylistic battle in France which opposes the intolerant, fanatical defenders of New Orleans jazz *to the exclusion of all others* (my italics) against those true jazz fans with a wider view, who remain open to discussion and do not limit themselves to any one style (no matter how interesting), is nothing compared to the one currently raging in America. Over there they do not merely whistle and hoot through concerts of which they disapprove, they write large-format, heavy 400-page books to prove their point.

These books are often not uninteresting and I have just finished rereading one of them: *Shining Trumpets* by Rudi Blesh – which gave me the idea for this column, starting with my title. There is no doubt that such works provide an insight into the nature of intolerance (this is certainly not aimed personally at Rudi Blesh, whose books have many attributes and who is in any case entitled to his own opinions) and statements like those he aims at Duke Ellington are food for thought.

Page 134: '. . . The absurd, pretentious and hybrid works of Duke Ellington and other so-called "modern jazz" musicians are nothing but vulgar aberrations, travesties of the creative black American genuis . . .'

58

Page 239: '. . . The orchestral efforts of a certain Duke Ellington are often, and quite erroneously, considered jazz . . .'

Page 281: '. . . Speaking about jazz, Ellington has never played it.'

Blesh is of course correct, in the sense that he is careful to begin with such a narrow definition of 'jazz' that nothing will fit into it other than marching bands and that music called 'New Orleans'. Louis Armstrong himself barely makes it. He uses examples which fit his thesis – Ellington works like 'Black, Brown and Beige' and 'Reminiscing in Tempo' which redefine jazz – and conveniently ignores all of the other Ellington records any traditional jazz collector would be proud to own.

I do not intend or pretend to say all there is to say about Ellington in a few lines. Personally I consider him a towering figure, which obviously implies that I do not exactly agree with Blesh. But in effect what Blesh will not recognize is that Duke has succeeded in writing on paper all sorts of polyphonic, polyrhythmic, harmonic (and any other 'ic' you might mention) passages which leave those you find even on good collectively improvised records far behind. You are free to like them or not, I hasten to add. But to refuse to admit that a man can improvise for seventeen musicians (which is what Duke does) is to refuse to allow him to be himself. And only to appreciate something when it is created spontaneously and by chance is the musical equivalent of sitting monkeys in front of typewriters and waiting for them to write, by chance, *Remembrance of Things Past*.

My analogy is of course false. Because New Orleans musicians know very well what they must play, what rules to follow, they are not monkeys. But then where's the improvisation? And how is Ellington any different?

BEBOP TIME

(*Combat*: 20/21 June, 1948)

Since bebop has become such a topical subject, everybody has naturally become a bebopper. But despite all the talk, very few people are capable of answering when you ask them point-blank: 'Just how is bebop different from the jazz that preceded it?' I made several vague attempts to define it a few months ago, but ended up confining myself to the opinion of critics I consider authorities on the subject. Technical analysis does not fall within my province. I try to be a revealer rather than an adjective (ex: the clown of Montauban).*

Well now, I was recently asked to translate an article by Ross Russell for *Jazz Hot* magazine. Russell owns Dial, a small independent jazz record company, and has little by little come to love bebop and to specialize in the genre. Russell deals with certain elements which are not uninteresting.

One of the first, and not least amusing, is the following. Russell remarks that though European musicians were capable of assimilating the melodic elements of bebop with amazing rapidity, they have failed totally when it comes to the rhythm

---

Translator's note: critic Hugues Panassié, who lived in that village during the Occupation.

section, the subject of his étude. And the reason is very simple. The ride cymbal is the central element of bebop drumming. Russell maintains that the frequency of cymbal vibration is the same as that type of noise known as 'white noise'. He does not define just exactly what that frequency is but, if memory serves, I believe it is somewhere between five and six thousand vibrations per second. Record-playing machines being generally designed to filter out that noise, the cymbal is filtered at the same time and so we don't hear it on recordings at all.

That being said, here are the other essential elements of bebop drumming.

First of all, the general objective is to produce a flowing legato by continually keeping the 4/4 time on the ride cymbal. The bass drum is used for varied irregular accents rather than to play four beats to the bar. The other hand and foot are free to attack the snare drum, tom-tom and the other cymbals.

What has happened is that, to quote Russell: 'By moving the basic beat from the bass drum to the ride cymbal, the modern drummer has done more than produce a new timbre and a new "beat", he has arrived at a new and remarkable economy of means.'

According to Russell, bebop involves polyrhythms to a previously unimagined extent and these polyrhythms are produced by the drummer alone. The bass must anchor the time (Russell says that the mistake of bebop bassists coming out of older styles is to play behind the beat, which was acceptable only so long as the bass drum kept the 4/4 going).

I trust that all my readers are now prepared to listen to bebop recordings with new ears.

The Latest Platters

(*Combat*: 27/28 June, 1948)

I have taken the liberty of borrowing this pithy expression from American disc jockeys, who have at least twenty ways to describe today's subject: newly released records.

Let's begin with Pathé-Marconi's 'His Master's Voice'. 'Oop Pop a Da' and 'Ow', marvellous recordings by Dizzy Gillespie with almost the same band we heard in Salle Pleyel. Listening to this record still another time, I could not help but think of Everybody's Lord and Master, Hugues Panassié who, leaving the above-mentioned concert, commented to Roncin, of the Hot Club d'Angers: 'I love jazz . . .'

Well, personally I don't love jazz but I certainly do adore this record. 'Oop Pop a Da' starts with a couple of measures which could at the very least be described as tormented. Then a short piano solo (ah, those solos by John Lewis while Dizzy does his funny little dance in front of his band) leading into a vocal duet in which Kenneth Hagood and Dizzy converse with humour. Their vocal is punctuated by a series of ensemble glisses, and Dizzy plays several sensational licks. All of which is impossible to analyse on paper. It is for ears only. The reverse side, 'Ow', is almost as good. Buy this record even if you can't pay your taxes and have to talk your girlfriend out of going to the movies . . .

Odéon brings us 'Our Delight' and 'Good Dues Blues' by Dizzy's big band along with 'I'm Lost' and 'Pet's Spring One' by the King Cole Trio and Fats Waller's 'I'm Crazy about My Baby' coupled with 'Draggin' My Heart Around'. All of these come out of the English Parlophone catalogue (this confusion of labels and masters will always remain a mystery to your humble collector). Every one of these discs is, in its own way, excellent. 'Our Delight' includes some of Dizzy's most beautiful recorded soloing, and 'Good Dues Blues' features a curious and interesting vocal.

The King Cole is delicious just like every King Cole.

As for Fats, I allow myself to pronounce the following axiom: 'No record by Fats Waller can be bad.' Recorded in 1931, this one has lost none of its punch. Fats and Erroll Garner are, until the New Order arrives, the best solo pianists around. Their left hands? I can't really say – I'm no technical expert.

After They've Gone

(*Combat*: 4/5 July, 1948)

May 23 marked the end of a 'Musical Memorial Week' in honour of the great jazz musician/composer/pianist Fats Waller. The *Pittsburgh Courier*, a large-circulation black weekly, devoted an entire page to a photo of Fats who, by the time he died at the age of thirty-nine, was credited with 450 songs.

Jazz fans are all familiar with the rough and buoyant voice of the most jocular singer in jazz history, and they are aware of the thanks we owe him for bringing us 'Honeysuckle Rose', 'Ain't Misbehavin'', 'Black and Blue' . . . the list is endless.

Fats died on 15 December, 1943. We never saw him here in the flesh. I began to understand the extent of our loss when *Stormy Weather*, that marvellous (for Hollywood, anyway) film was finally shown in Paris two years ago. But a quote by his co-composer Andy Razaf has just plunged me into even deeper despair:

> The public which applauded the master pianist, organist and composer, and the wonderful actor, never really had the opportunity to appreciate the fact that Fats hardly scratched the surface of his genius . . . I believe that if Fats had lived and had had the opportunity to spend more time developing

64

his creative talents, he would have contributed enormously to American music . . .

I tend to agree. There's no doubt that Fats had plenty of surprises in store for us. The perfection of some of his songs is obvious proof. But, still, it's not certain he could ever have brought more ambitious works to the attention of the public.

Take Duke Ellington, for example. Duke enjoys even a greater reputation than Fats. He has had the time and the opportunity to write whatever he likes.

Nevertheless, when he recorded 'Black, Brown and Beige', he was obliged to cut half of it; and an even better example, his 'Deep South Suite', one of his most ambitious compositions, is not available on record (there is only the V-disc made for the US armed forces from a live radio programme, and the master discs are probably lost by now), even though it was written quite a while ago. His opera, *Peter Ibbetson*, seems to have suffered a similar fate, and who knows what other material he has in the vault?

So, are we supposed to wait until Duke dies for his compositions to enter the general repertoire? Will producers continue to oblige him to record rehashed versions of his greatest hits? And all the while Duke is leading an orchestra which plays music completely compatible for the twelve-inch (even thirteen-inch) disc.

Doremi-sur-Seine

Nay-sayers will probably contend that 'Black, Brown and Beige' is not jazz. But 'Deep South Suite'? And 'Reminiscing in Tempo'? They're not jazz either, no doubt. The reality is that some works are beyond the understanding of certain people who prefer to denigrate them rather than admit their own ignorance.

Duke Ellington is in fact the very essence of all that is best in contemporary black music. (The readers of the *Pittsburgh Courier* are well aware of this. Far from crowning Stan Kenton, they have once more awarded Duke Ellington first place in that publication's annual poll.)

But the recording companies (except small labels incapable of battling the majors) think above all of how to sell their monstrosities, and provide financing only for projects that involve the Ninth Symphony with the chorus from Doremi-sur-Seine because Beethoven has been dead for a hundred years and is thus per se serious.

Our grandchildren will no doubt be able to buy a limited-edition album of 'Mood Indigo' interpreted by the saxophone quartet of the Garde Républicaine on the occasion of the hundredth anniversary of Duke's death.

P.S. An editing error distorted my quotation from the Master of Us All in my previous column. Everybody's Master Pain-ass-ié really said, as he came out of that Dizzy Gillespie concert: 'I love jazz, but that's not jazz . . .' The second half of the phrase was omitted. I want to set the record straight. It's a funny record.

SEND JAZZ BACK DOWN TO THE CAVES!

(*Combat*: 1/2 August, 1948)

The editorial in the July issue of the interesting American magazine *Record Changer* vehemently attacks 'concert-hall jazz'. It seems that, having arrived from the West Coast for a concert in Carnegie Hall, the Kid Ory band played to empty seats because of insufficient preparation and publicity.

The editorial speaks about acoustics, a point of interest to the Parisian jazz fan. Carnegie Hall is no better suited for the music than Salle Pleyel, its Parisian equivalent. A formation like Ory's – seven guys, three blowing through tubes and four banging or plucking on something – would be just as lost in Pleyel as the small combos of Don Redman, Rex Stewart and, even smaller, Duke Ellington, which recently played there. In the case of Duke, who is not known for his loud piano playing, it was annoying for listeners seated fifty metres away who, despite amplification, could not hear all there was to hear. On the other hand, in the first few rows, it was disconcerting to hear music coming from speakers above you to the left and the right rather than the stage. In addition, as the editorial correctly observes, accustomed to playing in smaller places, the musicians are themselves uncomfortable.

In Paris the problem is to be able to earn back the enormous investment involved in bringing jazz musicians across the Atlantic and paying them in dollars. This leads quite logically to larger venues. Obviously, the lucky people on the other side of the Atlantic do not suffer from the same scarcity of musicians with which we are forced to live, but the *Record Changer* article teaches us that when an orchestra like Kid Ory's comes to New York from California, it's almost like crossing the Atlantic. And to conclude on a sorry note, because this is vacation time, the saddest time of year, let us quote the editorial's conclusion.

When Ernie Anderson, the first serious promoter of jazz in concert halls, organized his 'Eddie Condon in Town Hall' concerts, he announced that he was going to take jazz out of cellars and smoky rooms. So the cellars were forced to close, while jazz remained extremely awkward on large air-conditioned stages. This brings us to the point – send jazz back to where it came from, and follow it.

Which, for someone like me, who loves to spend his nights in caves, is only stating the obvious.

Don't Lower Jazz to the Classical Level

(*Combat*: 29 October, 1948)

To reinaugurate this unperiodic column after holiday time, I would like to talk to my readers yet again about a subject close to my heart: jazz on stage. For a time at the beginning, jazz was a sport limited to dirty joints decorated with mirrors, and then to cabarets, dingy dives, nasty parlours and other places where people dance.

It was later at home for snobs in plush red-tapestry clubs before rising to the level of the boards, that is to say one and half metres above the orchestra seats. Progress led to more progress until, as the film *New Orleans* illustrates so astutely (!), the music has taken its place among the 'arts'. The time is not far away when the opera will hire Cab Calloway to play in the pit. Is this good or bad?

We come back to the ticklish problem of arranged jazz – from the danger of over-arranging to not enough or no arrangements at all.

The danger of over-arranging is that it will little by little lower jazz to the level of executed music, as opposed to the imaginative music it should be. And thereby lower jazz to the level of classical music.

On stage, the problem of no arranging at all is evident – the music is left to pure inspiration and if it happens to be lacking there's nothing left. In this case the music is anyway condemned from the start to communicate only with an elite group of initiates.

The solution, as I believe I've already said somewhere, consists of partially arranged jazz like Woody Herman's head charts. As I've also said, this unhappily has drawbacks of its own, principally to instil the musicians with lazy habits.

But that's not the strangest part.

For years now the critics have been trying to get jazz to be taken seriously at all costs. And little by little, they are getting there – in America concert jazz is increasingly successful. Kenton, Dizzy and Hampton are breaking attendance records all over the country. In France, jazz clubs are obviously dying out along with a renewed explosion of concerts. This is that 'savage music', mind you. And, voilà, the critics are delighted. But the more concerts there are, the less sincere jazz we hear. And the same critics insist on sincere jazz.

This is called, using the King's English (not to make a habit of it), a vicious circle.

Jazz and Peace

(*Combat*: 24 December, 1948)

Everybody is talking about an American named Gary Davis, who has some strange habits. He keeps tearing up his passport, which he says he no longer needs, while camping on the steps of the UN building in Paris. In addition he makes public appointments in the Vél' d'Hiv with people like our friend Comrade André Breton, who can be called nothing if not serious. It is not surprising that they all say war is ridiculous, and I'll move far to the left to agree with that. But when they declare themselves citizens of the world, I feel like telling them that there is already a large group of people who have been world citizens for a long time. They are called jazz fans.

Because if a real global village exists, it's populated by jazz fans of all ilks from India to Kamtchatka, from Japan to Australia (you could go on almost indefinitely). Jazz is called by the same name in every country on the planet, and the language is the same for anyone involved with it on any level: English.

And that's not all. Jazz records are made in every country you could name, and for a reason quite independent of the policies of multinational record companies. For example, certain marvellous Ellingtons from 1938–40 have been pressed in Australia. How did the masters arrive down there? It's a mystery. In any

71

case they're there.

Speak of Truman or Stalin to residents of the Cape of Good Hope and, if they're jazz fans, they will tell you that these people do not interest them ten per cent as much as Louis Armstrong or Coleman Hawkins – or Charlie Parker if they've been bitten by the bebop bug.

World government is being created in the form of an international jazz community – it's already created, in fact. Why are all these other people tiring themselves out talking about the subject?

He Who Wants to Can

(*Combat*: 14 January, 1949)

Antonin, one of my beloved readers, wrote a kind letter wishing me a happy new year (why didn't you think of that?), and took advantage of the occasion to ask my advice. 'I'm young,' he said, 'and I would like to learn to play a jazz instrument. Can you help me choose?'

Seeing as how I want to, and remembering the immortal words of Busch – 'he who wants to can' – I am going to give him some advice, what's more in public.

Generally speaking, the choice is as follows: the trumpet (or cornet); alto, tenor and baritone sax (plus, more rarely, soprano and bass); the clarinet; trombone; the rhythm instruments piano, bass, guitar and drums. Actually, certain freaks use other pieces of plumbing like the French horn, the finger piano, the electric violin and the jawbone of an ass. But we will limit our study to the first group, leaving the second for the weirdos.

The trumpet can be recommended only in that it involves having three dexterous fingers of one hand, the easiest part, and a certain labial muscular ability which can be developed painlessly during adolescence through practice with the little girl next door. Other than that, it's a nasty business, physically very tiring and full of unexpected quacks (called clinkers in the King's English).

73

Same problem with the trombone (slide or valve), only worse. But at least you can amuse yourself by imitating the sound of a calf braying for its mother.

The saxophone family (we include their forebear, that poor neglected cylinder the clarinet) has very attractive subtle and brilliant properties. I find this (alto or tenor) the ideal instrument for someone who feels he has a true jazzistic soul. One big problem: like the trumpet, you make the notes with your lips, which are placed on a fixed mouthpiece. Playing the saxophone, you are dependent upon a reed which is liable to sire an infinite number of winged creatures (in extreme cases, the duck-billed platypus). In any case, do not play clarinet, a frightful tool. Only Barney Bigard has ever been able to squeeze anything respectable out of one – Bechet also, although he's even better on soprano sax. Plus the clarinet sometimes goes beep-beep-beep.

Now for the rhythm instruments.

It is possible, once apprehension is subdued, to come to terms with the drums (bearing in mind the landlord's holidays). Drums are a combination of complex objects which, however, leave your voice free to sing lively refrains (this is why drummers are always appreciated by the ladies, to whom they whisper sweet little nothings while they play). Drums involve constantly moving hands and feet – very good exercise.

The guitar. The strings cut your fingers, and then you still have to make notes with them, like a violin – it's quite discouraging. But it can make you seem oh so charming.

Like drums, the bass is exhausting to carry when you go somewhere to play, and then you are persecuted by the other musicians who neither hear nor respect you. On the other hand you can hide ten kilos of chocolate in it when you come back across the border from Belgium.

The piano? Let's not even discuss it. Do you realize that there are eighty-eight keys for only ten fingers? Well, twenty counting the feet and twenty-one including the nose.

Nevertheless, Antonin, I advise you to play piano. You don't have to carry it anywhere, you can learn about harmony from it and, with the progress of electronics, ten years from now everything will have a piano keyboard, even ocarinas.

BILLY MAY AND HIS ORCHESTRA

Record Review: 'My Silent Love'; 'Fat Man Boogie'.

Despite my technologically advanced speakers with a fourteen-decibel tweeter and the woofer that goes down to minus six (engineers will know what I'm talking about), it was just about impossible for me to hear this record because it's all treble and no bass. But in addition to that (after all, maybe it's my lousy turntable), it's shameful, revolting and depressing to consider the fact that Billy May earned a million last year (this one too) by so blatantly copying the style of Jimmie Lunceford (with such little imagination). His ensembles are excellent, very together, but without a trace of commitment or one note that isn't copied, calculated, rehearsed and rehearsed again – this sort of thing even ruins Lunceford. Granted, it's good dance music. Just as if I copy *Le Misanthrope* and sign it Delaroche, it's still good theatre. There have always been forged Vermeers. The only original thing about Billy May is that he revived instrumental dance music. Thanks for that. But a few more ideas, m----(erde) alors!

MILES DAVIS: THE EARS OF A FAUN

(*Jazz News*: May, 1949)

The first thing that strikes you about Miles Davis is that he's really beautiful to look at. People tell me he's too short but that's a meaningless quibble. Studying his photographs, I've come to the conclusion that though he may be slightly more imaginative than sensual, both of these qualities are more or less well balanced with intellect. And though I'm not sure you can trust photographs in general, on one of them he appears to have the ears of a faun – which I find really nice.

It's impossible not to talk about yourself when you are a critic. This is only fair because otherwise saying 'this or that is such and such and there's no doubt about it' would add cowardice to the sin of assumed infallibility. All of which leads me to tell you that in my opinion Miles Davis's chorus on 'Now's the Time' is one of the best bebop solos of all time.

I said something similar about Ben Webster's chorus on Duke Ellington's 'Chlo-E' six years ago. Since then, I've finally managed to add 'Chlo-E' to my record collection. To tell the truth I do not yet have 'Now's the Time'. But I have pen-pals in New Zealand, Labrador and the United States and I'll get it sooner or later. In any case, I won't even have to listen to it because I already know Miles's chorus by heart.

In a strange way, this chorus essentially sums up his qualities (both technical excellence and personality traits):

a) First of all, constant total relaxation. I don't think it's possible to play more relaxed than Davis. He saunters as though in a flower garden in the month of May (beautiful image, if I do say so; you might get somewhere using the same phrase right now with your lady). Such easy confidence is quite reassuring.

b) In the second place, his articulation is absolutely flabbergasting. The spaces which suddenly appear in the middle of sinuous lines serve to relax (physically) and excite (intellectually) at the same time. Miles goes from note to note logically, creatively, precisely – he manages to take the listener somewhere totally new using soft, polished solid material like bricks in a potter's oven.

c) Third, a curious sound – nude, vulnerable, almost no vibrato, totally calm, but despite all that as excitingly vehement as Jonah Jones or Roy Eldridge. It's a monk's sound – somebody who is part of this century but who can look at it with serenity.

d) Finally, a sensational sense of rhythmic structure and well-tuned ears. Because to land on your feet like this gentleman after launching into such complex constructions takes a healthy sense of balance, you bet, my dear.

'Now's the Time' is not a complete inventory of Miles's capabilities. Listen to some of the tunes at breakneck tempos he executes with his fine-feathered friend Charlie Parker – you won't be disappointed. He makes it seem so easy, almost always in the middle register, but he can also be acrobatic when he feels like it. He can climb high and weave and bob fast. It's much easier to analyse Miles at half-speed. Also (parenthetically) it's more logical in general to judge a soloist playing a medium or slow tempo because it's much harder to impress people and a lot more difficult to be interesting let alone fascinating – for proof, listen to 'On the Sunny Side of the Street' by Lester Young to understand why he is such a profoundly great gentleman.

To come back to our friend Miles Davis, what more can I tell you? I'm absolutely overjoyed he's coming to play at the Pleyel Festival. I hope we'll hear him with his partner Charlie Parker, even though he is not currently a member of Charlie's quintet. Who knows?

CHARLIE PARKER: SUPERBIRD

(*Jazz Hot*: May, 1949)

We publish the following review without necessarily agreeing with it. It was written by a certain Baron Visi* who, while passing through Paris in April, claims to have heard the first set of Charlie Parker's 8 May concert. We trust this scoop will be of interest to our readers.

The excited and screaming crowd did not prevent me from hearing that lick . . . Charlie Parker's lick . . . the lick he had just improvised for us . . . before our very eyes . . . Wow! This man gives birth to such divine inspiration . . . this . . . how can I put it? . . . this superman . . . one of the gods come to visit us on earth . . . but why limit him to just one of many? . . . this God. This , . . . God and a half!

Holy Charlie!

That lick of his, you must have noticed it, how could you miss it?

G, E, F, G, C, B, A, G, F, D, A, E, G, D, D . . .

Oh Dear Lord in Heaven if only I had the Gothic ardour of

Translator's note: anagram of Boris Vian.

someone like George Olde-Groove* so I could shower all the praise he deserves on Our Master Parker ... to describe how his Holy Light knocked all of those late-blooming Sunday drivers into the aisles.

I want to immortalize that lick.

For eternity.

Did you see how he played it? Ah! Twentieth-century man is too limited to appreciate the sensibilities of this genius whose relevance spans all of eternity.

(Actually I seem to be able to come up to Olde-Groove's level after all. But I did pluralize 'sensibility', and that key 'ies' perhaps illustrates how different my Gothic ardour is from his.)

We are dealing here with a concept which is too far above the intellectual limitations our atrophied century has placed on music. (Some of you may be aware that I have stolen that sentence from page 51 of *The Real Jazz Music* by a certain promising young critic named Hugues Panassié, but never mind.)

Bud Freeman is a strange musician (op cit).

But let us return to our irresistible Charlie.

The C is the key to the entire harmonic construction of the lick. The alto sax cannot be compared to the piano, since with ten fingers and one mouth you can play only one note at a time. A piano can produce ten or twelve (twenty or twenty-five with an elbow, and almost the entire keyboard if your feets too big). But on the saxophone – I repeat, alto saxophone – the C must be transposed because it's an E-flat instrument (by way of a perfidious A), and the ear hears that the sound falls exactly between F-sharp and A-flat and that it's really a G. Now Charlie played that same lick in 'Fuckin' the Bird', a tune in D-flat diminished, and don't forget the transposition. The absolute value, that is to say in relation to the following notes, we can more or less consider to be C. That's the essential.

'Personally, I consider the Swede Bob Lane to be one of the best white pianists' (Panassié, op cit, p. 135).

An E follows the C in Charlie's solo. Do you understand the undeniable inevitability with which the E connects the C preceding it to the following F? The true greatness of a musician

---

*Respected jazz critic.

can be appreciated through such bursts of eloquence. There are of course other examples, though it is this particular one that interests us for the moment.   · ·

'This entire rich vein of ideas would be meaningless if Duke's orchestra did not know how to frame it properly' (Panassié, op cit, p. 177).

Then, after the F (and here's the really incredible moment about which one could say, without exaggeration, Charlie is a genius – *the* genius) . . . after the F, Charlie goes back to the G.

If you cannot comprehend this through words, try humming it . . . G, E, F, G. There it is. That's it . . . ze grouve, ze cozmic grouve.

Wow! That second G!

And that's not all . . .

N.D.L.R. But that will *have* to be all, for now at least. The abundance of Baron Visi's material forces us to postpone the following instalment of this review until the next issue. The first section, consecrated to Charlie Parker's first chorus, takes up ninety-two double-spaced typed manuscript pages. We ask the reader to accept our apologies.

DUKE ELLINGTON: CATALYST OR VAMPIRE?

(*Combat*: 4 February, 1949)

There is such a difference of scope between Duke Ellington and all other jazz musicians that you might wonder: why even bother mentioning the others? The fact remains that one does talk about the others, myself included, even though I have nothing to say. But to return to Duke, this is something many people ponder – when a musician joins Duke's band, he is framed with such extraordinary richness that if he does not become famous after a certain time it must really be his own fault.

Does playing with Duke develop the intrinsic talents of each musician (playing arrangements of such quality with such a quality orchestra must be like finding yourself smack-dab in the middle of a harem), or does the Ellington orchestra owe its quality to the fact that Duke co-opts the individual virtues of each member?

In short, is Duke a catalyst or a vampire? There is, however, a third possibility: perhaps he simply has the nose of a hunting dog, sniffing out the sort of fine players he needs. But has Cootie Williams done anything better than 'Concerto for Cootie' or 'Echoes of Harlem' since he left Duke? And Barney Bigard? (an even better example). Ben Webster? – not such an easy question because some of his small-band recordings are more than just good, and rumour has it that Ben is going to rejoin Duke's band. So. Catalyst? Hard to say unless you're in the band yourself. What part does the orchestra's team spirit play? Ask yourself the question. Try to find the answer. In any case whatever you come up with, here's an exception to prove the rule: Jimmy Hamilton, Duke's current clarinettist and one of Benny Goodman's victims, is so annoying that it can be said without qualification that he brings nothing to Duke and Duke can do nothing for him.

PILLORY REX STEWART

(*Combat*: 18 February, 1949)

The title is the thesis – he deserves it.

I'd be surprised if jazz is a subject that ever makes the front page of *Combat*. Nevertheless, the large number of fans who crowd into the Théatre Edouard VII every week for the 'Jazz Parade' series encourages me to insist on the news value of the most recent concert – Sunday, 13 February.

Here's the situation in a nutshell. It was an excellent first half, which featured highly talented young musicians (Jean-Claude Fohrenbach, tenor sax; Maurice Meunier, clarinet; Eddy Bernard, piano; Claude Marty, drums; Jack Smaley, bass; and Aubert on guitar – I name them because, in context, they actually deserve more attention than the 'star' Rex Stewart, who is the subject of this article and who literally ruined the performances of his colleagues).

In the second half, Rex appeared with fellow trumpeters the black American Bill Coleman and Frenchman Aimé Barelli – three trumpets with one rhythm section, Bill Coleman's rhythm section, probably the best in Paris at the moment, consisting of Bernard Peiffer, piano; Jean Bouchéty, bass; Roger Paraboschi, drums.

They opened with a superb arrangement of 'Lady be Good',

which put everybody 'in the mood'. Unfortunately, not only did this tune bring out the best in Coleman and Barelli, who were a bit too strong for Stewart – he does not like competition – but the audience also demonstrated its approval of Peiffer and the rhythm section. From then on, to the end of this second set, Rex did everything possible to attract attention to himself – God knows he can be a clown when he wants to. But on Sunday his selfishness went too far. He brought everybody down – Coleman, Barelli, the section – and as far as his own playing was concerned . . . I dislike having to badmouth a musician whose recordings (those he made with Ellington) are among the most beautiful of all time, but the trumpeter called Rex Stewart just wasn't there.

It was sabotage. He appointed himself chief (if there was one at all, it should have been Bill), slapped Peiffer on the back and made funny faces while the pianist, as always, tried to play his best; then he grabbed Paraboschi's drumsticks and coerced Barelli into banging them on a conveniently located column. And that's not half of it. The most shameless histrionics, distressing insolence and complete caddishness, along with the least musical trumpet playing (I'm being generous) you can possibly imagine – last Sunday, Rex Stewart demonstrated all of those things.

If the producers of the 'Jazz Parade' would be so kind as to consider my opinion, not at all an isolated opinion, they should systematically boycott Rex. This gentleman simply has too much ego for the poor musicians who play with him. Rex is going to lose not only their audience, but their performers as well. Obviously, I would hesitate to say all this – certainly to write it – if this was America. But Rex has the bad luck to have come to a country without systematized racial prejudice. That's why I allow myself to tell him, man to man: 'Mister Stewart, you have conducted yourself like a monkey.' I'm sorry, there's no other word for it.

One Hundred and Seventy-eight Blowers

(*Combat*: 6 May, 1949)

More and more jazz fans (real ones who play records, not those who collect them to decorate their walls) are enjoying the stylistic squabbles between various Hot Clubs, jazz-record companies and the nasty madmen who make their living writing on all these people about whom the man-in-the-street doesn't care one jot anyway.

Not that I pretend to speak in the name of Joe Blow. I pardon his strong and perfectly understandable taste for military marches, Polish polkas and accordion waltzes to go along with his sausage and bottle of red wine. In any case, were it not for these alley-fights (above) we would never have been able to experience the big blowout last Wednesday at the Lido Cabaret.

Mr Pierre-Louis Guérin, the producer of next week's jazz festival, brought journalists and musicians together – a commendable gesture – to offer them sandwiches and champagne and to allow the former to speak of the latter with that extreme competence uniquely endowed on French reporters. And so we witnessed this ear-tingling spectacle: blues played consecutively by Hubert Fol, Jacques Diéval and Don Byas (three 'modernists'), followed by Braslavsky (rabidly old-style), then Villers,

Meunier and Vernon (modernism-revisited), Claude Luter (the oldest of the old), terminating with Barelli and the Lido big band directed by René Leroux. And finally, the extraordinary out-chorus when all of them played the riffs together.

Ah! What a moving experience. How comforting it was to hear all those diversely loyal hearts beat once and for all in unison, while our friend Paraboschi beat like a deaf man on a bongo which was close by, thanks to one of those coincidences which often places musical tools near musichanics (or musicians as they are more commonly called).

So it seems that mutual hatred is a thing of the past. I propose a slogan for the coming festival: 'New Orleans, birthplace of Bipope', or perhaps: 'In togetherness lies strength'. This happy new state of affairs strikes me as reflecting perfect taste and form. It makes me feel just wonderful.

Festival Small Talk

(*Combat*: 13 May, 1949)

The Salle Pleyel Festival's Monday and Tuesday concerts were consecrated, respectively, to bebop and Sidney Bechet. I won't rehash the high points of these two events since they were both broadcast through the good offices of Radio France, which (how could you ever have doubted it?) now appears to be wide-open to all kinds of jazz.

I would, however, like to serve up some food for thought by commenting on what might be called auxiliary aspects of the festival.

Why was Carlo Krahmer's band received with such reticence when it plays on a level which, I'm sure, is not really below that of the other young white European groups? It seems to me that if Krahmer had had the chance to play with Sidney Bechet who, despite his wonderful sound and enormous talent, still plays popular music, Krahmer would have been as well received as Luter, whose incontestible attributes I do not for a moment question but whose faults I cannot, on the other hand, ignore. And how do you explain the enormous success of Graeme Bell here? Carlo is not any worse than Bell. It's important to point out that when you watch Bechet rehearse, you realize that one session with a leader of his inexhaustible patience and unequalled competence would be enough to raise the level of any young musician. We should further mention that English jazz musicians are cut off from current developments in black jazz because of the deplorable policy of their union, run by classical musicians, which forbids work permits for foreign instrumentalists – so any possible resulting backwardness isn't entirely their fault.

To continue the small talk, did you know that Miles Davis had never heard Bechet before? He said Bechet reminds him a lot of Johnny Hodges. Which isn't dumb when you think about it.

Miles engineered a delightful coup Tuesday night. A hysterical young female fan ran out of the hall and flung herself at him with a photo to autograph. She had cut one of Hot Lips Page out of *Jazz News* and pasted it in the evening's programme. Without hesitation, Miles signed 'Oran "Hot Lips" Page, sincerely . . .'

When I saw this enthusiast make eyes at Miles and turn the page, I said to myself: 'She finally recognized him.'

But there was another photo of Lips on that page, this time next to one of Miles. And Miles signed 'Lips', again, under Lips's photo. Lips had a good laugh when Miles told him about it.

Eddy Bernard had his photo taken with Big Chief Moore – the most beautiful flowing beard next to the fattest Indian chief in the world. It's a scoop. I'll send a copy to all my female readers who ask nicely enough.

PRIDE AND PREJUDICE

(*Combat*: 14/15 May, 1949)

The mentality of amateur jazz musicians deserves in-depth investigation. The Pleyel Festival was a good place to observe this fascinating phenomenon for those who are interested in the question. Many more or less predictable events brought to mind conscious, or unconscious as the case may be, reactions.

I believe I've captured the heart of the matter by naming this article 'Pride and Prejudice'.

Concerning pride, I hasten to say that the word applies only to a category of amateurs with some minimum musical knowledge, and that on the other hand the majority of them do not have much about which to be proud. In fact the majority deserve to be hung for excess pride, and I will now introduce them to you.

Not long after arriving in Paris, Sidney Bechet told me, astonished: 'It's funny, you know, over here amateur jazz musicians never ask me to come and hear them, they ask me "where can I hear you play?"' The fact is that a large number of young people, intelligent and modest though they may be, do not want anything more than to listen to somebody else's pleasing improvisations. The more active minority, on the other hand, are the exact opposite.

When they are not working, professional musicians often get

89

together for impromptu jam sessions. What is the reaction of a likable young amateur in this case? He sits down and listens.

Unhappily, there always seem to be one or two others who will jump in and play with joyous insensitivity. You might think that after a little while they would just let it go and stop being assholes. But no – they play one miserable chorus after another and refuse to stop until all the other musicians around them leave. It obviously excites these people to play with Lips Page or Kenny Dorham. But meanwhile listeners are bored to death suffering through a dozen choruses by Mister Nobody in order to hear one by Max Roach.

I realize it's a delicate question. It's not easy to tap Nobody, who thinks he's hot stuff, on the back and tell him: 'You must be tired. Why don't you go have a taste?' Because he's going to answer: 'For once I have the chance to play with these guys . . . I'm not going to give it up. Why don't you bring me a cognac?'

Let's be blunt. When the best black American musicians like Don Byas, Roach, Dorham or Miles Davis play . . . if the band includes a white pianist because Tadd Dameron isn't free, or a white bassist if Tommy Potter doesn't feel like playing, fine. Bravo! It's only normal. But for goodness' sake let Zebird take a chorus once in a while.

American News

(*Combat*: 30 May, 1949)

American magazines have annoyed me too often with their extravagant praise of white bands to pass up this opportunity to rejoice over Michael Levin's magnificent put-down of Artie Shaw on the front page of *Down Beat* (20 May, 1948).

You have to give Mr Artie Shaw credit. He had the nerve to pretend to play, with forty musicians in a cabaret called Bop City, serious music. Prokofiev, no doubt. Or the dubious machinations of Nickie Belozowsky, or (more likely) Morton Gould and Pierre Potboiler.

'There has never in the history of music been such a pitiful bandleader,' wrote Mix (Levin's nom de guerre). His slashing criticism of the performance makes you feel almost sorry for Artie Shaw: 'Phrasing was stiff and sterile and there was no real emotion or intelligence as Shaw interpreted the works of Ravel and Debussy, composers who require subtlety and grace, with the same heavy hand as the rest of his programme – with clinkers, shaky rhythm and defective intonation.'

Don't tell me you think that's a bit hard on Mr Shaw. Only in France are there still any number of people who consider him a jazz musician – and, voilà, now we discover he's not a musician, period.

91

'Happily,' *Down Beat* continued, 'the same concert featured Ella Fitzgerald, who was in wonderful form – she was obviously what the paying public had come to hear.'

Now for some more American news. A sensational Miles Davis record has apparently just been released. The instrumentation is as follows: trumpet, trombone, alto, tenor,* French horn, tuba and three rhythm. Apparently it sounds marvellous and is superbly recorded in addition. And if I tell you there is also a certain Max Roach on drums . . .

Our old friend Erroll Garner continues to record apparently everywhere at the same time – Savoy, Modern, who knows where else. Just reading the reviews makes my mouth water. Patience. The Savoys will be released here soon. I hope. As far as the others are concerned, I'll figure out a way to get them somehow. All these records can lead you to the brink of bankruptcy.

I've already received many letters asking me, as I must admit I proposed (it's really my own fault), for the photo of Eddy Bernard and Big Chief Moore side by side. More patience. I'm taking care of it. They have to be printed before I mail them, n'est-ce pas?

Translator's note: it was a baritone.

REFLECTIONS ON TIME AND SPACE WITH AN EMPTY HEAD

(Combat: 10 June, 1949)

I believe I've already complained here about the unfortunate size of the Atlantic Ocean which, in the realm of jazz, puts ten years between the date of creation in America and assimilation in Europe. What better example than the recent case of Sidney Bechet? Young people over here are only now realizing that ten years ago Sidney Bechet was already a great man.

I've also said (I'm very talkative) that the record companies bear some of the responsibility for this. It's time for them to try (and if not 'them', why not some new ones) to get out of their rut. But that's another story.

You know one place where all this has led? Young people who feel more or less close to the New Orleans style have rushed to buy those rare soprano saxophones which can be found in French music stores. (Bechet plays the soprano saxophone.) The situation is so bad that Selmer has no more sopranos in stock; there's a waiting-list and it's even impossible to find one to rent.

Worse!

The people who already play the instrument love to quote a

passage from Dvořák's 'Humoresque' in the middle of 'Careless Love'. They squeeze in a few bars of 'Strangers in the Night' anywhere at all. But why do they stop at that point? Why not take it as far as Bechet? Bechet frequently plays 'Laura' for his own amusement. I'll inform those readers who are not up to date on such inside information that Bechet playing 'Laura' is almost as weird as Louis Armstrong playing 'La Vie en Rose'. Oh well, maybe ten years from now . . .

Enough nastiness.

Learn the soprano sax. Work, make an effort.

After ten years, you might discover that a very talented individual named Johnny Hodges played the alto sax in a cultivated manner from 1930–49. This instrument is not so chic at the moment. You might also learn that Harry Carney illustrated what great grace can be coaxed out of that outsized tool called the baritone. And that a certain Tricky Sam Nanton did some beautiful things on the slide trombone which you never heard in a marching band. I could go on . . .

But what's the point? After all, Tricky Sam died only a short while ago and, I repeat, Hodges and Carney have only twenty years with Ellington to their credit. Much too soon for France.

Anyway time has nothing to do with it, and this article, written with an empty head and no deep thought, does not prove anything.

PARKER AND THE CUBANS

(*Combat*: 11 July, 1949)

I'm very annoyed because I just received a package of beautiful records from 'Noo Yawk', among them some Charlie Parker with Machito (a rumba band) and I wanted to talk to you about them to make you drool with desire. But bad luck. We are all aware that we no longer have to suffer electricity cuts; now they call them local circuit breakdowns.

So I haven't been able to listen to these records and cannot talk about them. Guarding my well-known integrity, I won't give an opinion without precise research. Meanwhile, at least I can say that the records are scheduled to be released in France in the near future. If the electricity doesn't come on soon, perhaps you'll hear them before I do. Then you can tell me about them.

Let's take advantage of this breakdown to say how depressing record collecting can be. Of the twenty-five or thirty items in this package, there are at least six companies of which I've never heard. They have beautiful red, green and blue labels – Aristocrat, Sittin'inurth, Bandwagon, Trophy, Staff, etcetera. It's nauseating, worse than stamp collecting . . . wait a minute, the vacuum cleaner's happy song tells me the juice is back on.

Well, I have to tell you how much I love the feeling of these four Machito sides, one of which features Flip Phillips and the

95

other three Charlie Parker. It's not the first time that jazz has been put together with Cuban rhythms. Remember Louis's 'Peanut Vendor'? That was already something. And Ellington's 'Conga Brava' and 'Flaming Sword' – I consider the latter one of Duke's masterpieces. In France we always hear Cuban rhythms distorted by the working-class taste for easy melodies. In reality it's one of jazz's richest roots, as important as boogie-woogie but infinitely richer.

I can hear people crying 'heresy'. These are the same people who never protest when military marches are camouflaged as dance tunes, and who say that Duke Ellington is over the hill when they hear 'Black, Brown and Beige'.

One of the tunes Charlie Parker plays with Machito is called 'Okiedoke'. Need I say more? And it's bizarre to hear Zebird fly in more rigid formation than usual. Finally, if you want my opinion, these are very good records . . . Patience, they too will come . . .

MACHITO AND HIS ORCHESTRA UNDER THE DIRECTION OF CHICO O'FARRILL

Record Review: Afro Cuban Jazz Suite

You are probably aware of how much I like Machito's band and above all his rhythm section. You have also read about my love for Charlie Parker. Well here they are, together again, with Buddy Rich and Flip Phillips, for this astonishing 'Jazz Suite' by Chico O'Farrill, who wrote, arranged and directed this performance. Here are all the elements of real jazz, plus other elements besides, and if it's a bit hybrid, and not as brilliant as Ellington can be, it has its own personality and does not stay, thank God, on the old well-trodden paths. You'll find Parker and Flip stretching out, hear Buddy Rich pushing Machito's band to swing even harder than usual. Above all, you'll hear an LP which is really long-playing and not just a collection of three-minute segments. It's awesome music and if you don't think it's 'real' jazz, that's your problem. Because I love Louis and Hawkins, but I also love *Wozzeck* and Ravel's 'La Valse' and Machito – more than ever when he's with Parker – and now go back and reread the beginning of this because rather than talk a blue streak I'd rather listen to the record again . . .

97

Nut Season

(*Jazz News*: November, 1949)

This is autumn, nut season. That is why the directors of *Jazz News*, opportunists as always, have asked me to assume, henceforth and until otherwise notified, the duties of editor (in chief) of this funny-book which, it seems, will now become a boxing magazine. I am certainly not opposed to the distribution of nuts provided they're not coming towards me. Being a coward and a hypocrite, I'll find other targets.

Happily, there are enough jazz magazines – not to mention interested mass-market publications, books and radio programmes – to provide a large stock of bread in the cupboards of all the people who write about jazz. And the older bread gets the harder it hits.

So! There will be some changes made.* First, we will limit the number of our mistakes by reducing thought-provoking articles to a minimum. There are already too many such infuriating publications. As soon as possible we are going to

---

*The design of this page was laid out during a game of 'trou-madame' by the director, the local fire chief and the hard-hitting editor-in-chief's ninth auxiliary under-secretary.
(Nota bene: the janitor won.)

98

introduce a detachable filing-system of technical information which allows you to catalogue your records with considerable efficacy, and we will make sure to eschew criticism in favour of analysis. I can really talk when I want to, can't I? After that it will be our policy to run photos of pretty girls because that will brighten things up and because we must maintain our reputation as eroto-maniacs. And finally . . . you'll see for yourself. If I tell you everything in advance you won't buy the magazine.

The editor-in-chief welcomes appointments with female readers.

High-powered People

Hugusse Pain-ass-ié, a not quite jazz critic, has doubts about bebope

(Jazz News: November, 1949)

Whatever you do, don't say that Ansermet and Goffin are the real fathers of jazz criticism. Although it's certain that the latter's book was written in 1931, and Misters Coeuroy and Schaeffner dealt with the subject as early as 1926 (the former should have quit right there), it was actually Pain-ass-ié who discovered jazz all by himself, not Buddy Bolden as is sometimes believed.

I will not attempt to outline the career, packed with world-shattering genius, of this miraculous critic who has, lacking knowledge about anything else, single-handedly raised felicitous opinions about Saint Mezzerola to the level of an art form. I am going to deal only with the most recent flights of fancy by this man, a great among the greatest of the least great, whose fabrications, you'll have to admit, redefine the limits of the sordid.

Ah, poor Pain-ass-ié, bebope keeps him awake at night. And

he dumps on us, massacres, vilifies and vituperates because of it. While his personal mob echoes him and bands together to support him. (It does not surprise me that it includes contributors to this magazine, nor does their feeblistic intellectual level; I am surprised only by their number.)

How does the Prophet operate?

It's very simple.

Copying my system which earned me great praise and which I honed to perfection in *Jazzote* Magazine in 1912, he publishes carefully 'translated' and meticulously mutilated texts ... you must certainly realize how, doing this sort of thing, you can make people say absolutely anything you want them to.

What a rascal, right? The little bastard ...

It is obvious that he has no subjective prejudice against bebope. It just exists, and he only has to know it exists. Because he never listened to it. It exists, mind you, but only in his imagination.

And to exorcize his fear of it, he hides behind names like Bechet, King Cole and Louis Armstrong. There he feels on solid ground, and he's sure to win the approval of everybody else who knows nothing about the music.

Note in passing that you can make a musician say whatever you want. You just have to know how to ask the right questions.

Recently, Pain-ass-ié began to get a little nervous about it. And so he spent a great many doubloons travelling to the States to be reassured.

'Maybe when you get right down to it,' he thought, 'there just might be a little something to this infernal bebope after all. Lester Young used to be such an awful musician ten years ago and listen to him now, he's wonderful – he must be wonderful, I said so myself; twice. So maybe bebope ... maybe the same thing will happen. What do you think, Madeleine?'

Madeleine could not reply. She was busy translating a blues into Javanese for Hugusse's next article.

'You see,' explained Hugusse: 'Mezzerola says it's no good. What better authority? But here in France, they don't seem to like Mezzerola very much any more! Ah, it was so easy with Mezzerola, he dictated and I wrote. But he's a little burned out; Luter plays better than he does. He's no longer so solid. I need a crushing argument – Armstrong, of course, Armstrong. Come on, let's go and see Armstrong. Who knows . . . interviewing other people with my well-known astute questions . . . maybe we'll get the right answers yet . . .'

So Madeleine packed their bags, they took the plane and for a year after that he could write that the deze, demz and dozes who defend bebope are idiots.

Bebope does not even exist. The devil himself, Charlie Parker, said so. Even he recognizes it.

But Pain-ass-ié is like Don Quichote – he's always Vianly fighting windmills.

It occurs to me that perhaps I am being too hard on Pain-ass-ié. I could certainly make some serious points if I tried hard, but it's hard indeed to take him seriously. One more thing. Every time I talk about Pain-ass-ié, he calls me a pornographer. Which is in fact his own fault. It would certainly be impossible to be pornographic speaking of Saint Catherine. And in addition he accuses me of defiling blacks. This time this was obviously unavoidable because I just summarized his own article.

PS: He's *always* insulting me. But how can I get back at him? It's impossible to insult a walking insult.

BIG AND LITTLE NEWS

(*Jazz News*: November, 1949)

– If you find this issue of *Jazz News* idiotic, buy the next one. It will be even worse.

– Elections for the post of Vice Pope of jazz will be held shortly in Paris. Write to *Jazz News* for information. Enclose a self-addressed envelope with two stamps so we can keep one of them.

– The badge of honour for the most stupid jazz article of the month goes to M. Montabré of *Le Figaro*. As always, *Jazz News* does not take part in this competition.

– A future issue will include a comprehensive simplified clarinet method invented by Saury (Maxime) of the University of Wisconsin.

– With regard to the pocket trumpet, the Americans have put a new elliptical mouthpiece on the market. According to the publicity, it will add three notes to the upper register. What should we do with them? We will be grateful to our readers for any suggestions.

– After deliberating for thirty-nine consecutive hours, the police department and the Minister of Fine Arts have rejected a proposal made by our colleagues at *Jazz Hot* in favour of a suggestion from the tenor saxophonist Jean Ledru, who wanted to replace the obelisk on the Place de la Concorde by a large column of air. Sculptor Ralph Schecroun, who had been proposed to execute the project, resigned from the Social and Moral Action Cartel upon learning of their decision.

– One good deed deserves another.

– Le Frisco, which opened its doors on rue Notre-Dame-de-Lorette with Kenny Clarke's band featuring Hubert Fol, Bill Coleman and James Moody, closed shortly thereafter. The cause is not known but we believe the prices were too high and the personnel too unfriendly for a place where people come to listen to jazz.

Louis Armstrong played in Salle Pleyel on Thursday and Friday, 3 and 4 November – and the 5th and 6th in the Théatre des Champs Elysées. Since two and two make four, there were four concerts. The programmes were pretty much the same, differing only in details. The concert of the 5th was the least satisfactory because of some untimely amplification problems; several cables broke down and who knows what else. Taken as a whole, these concerts were expensive entertainment: it cost 700 francs for the right to climb up to the second balcony.

The concerts in question bring several thoughts to mind. I have no intention of criticizing Armstrong, who sounded exactly as you'd expect from a man who has worked too hard in an exhausting number of performances throughout Europe. He played well enough but it was obvious that he paced himself carefully (with the exception of 'Muskrat Ramble' on the 6th, when we heard the Louis of the gold old days). If he has lost some power in his prodigious upper register, his attack remains clean and his sound is still pure. When he sings, however, he has that old feeling and his voice continues to reflect the complete Louis. Finally, Armstrong has a formidable stage presence; as an actor he has no peers. He'd be interesting even if he did nothing but stand there.

On the other hand, except for Earl Hines and Cozy Cole (pianist and drummer), who are perfection personified, Louis's orchestra left something to be desired. Though he swings well enough, bassist Arvell Shaw should improve his intonation. Regarding Teagarden and Bigard, let's just say bluntly that Tommy Dorsey and Benny Goodman would have been just as good. Their feeling was as cold as their technique was excellent, which does not add up to enough. And Teagarden's singing remains inconsistent and uninteresting.

I do not believe that the singer (*sic*) Velma Middleton sang one note in tune during the four evenings. And she makes a spectacle of herself playing the fool. She lacks the grace and humour of the Peters Sisters (which proves that corpulence is not the problem). She overdoes it and it's embarrassing.

The best moments? Those rare Louis solos, the accompaniment of Earl Hines and the consistent support of Cozy Cole, whose precision and dependability is unbeatable.

JAZZ IS DANGEROUS

'The Physiopathology of Jazz' by Freddy Flabby: (ex-psychiatric patient, insurance company doctor, Thursday painter and war hero)

(*Jazz News*: November, 1949)

Way back in antiquity, you find examples of the effect of the sclerosist and necrosant influence of jazz on living cells and the macromolecules of cytoplasm. When the walls of Jericho were blown down by Joshua's blaring trumpet, the traumatism infiltrated the thickness of the stone – and we understand that it produced, a fortiori, in this material which is much more delicate than the protoplasma humaine, pathological problems comparable to those which engender the most deadly passions like love of absinthe or la recherche de l'absolu (delirium tremens, paralysie général).

The work of Dr René Theillier dealing with lesions provoked by the 'repetition of the same impulse' brings to mind the danger of any music with constant rhythm. Jazz is the most common example, and so it is imperative that the power structure finally make up its mind to lance the wound and find a

106

cure for the galloping psychopathia that seems to be seizing hold of today's young people.

If we looked through a peep-hole and observed a puppy listening to a series of recordings of this 'primitive' music, we would find, after dedicating months to it, that large lesions of necrosity and greasy degenerence are produced in the historilogic of the cortex and the médullo surrénales. Thus hyperplasted, the subject loses its physiological activity and is destabilized by high winds – and you can imagine the hormonal and vagosympathetic destabilization which can follow, because nature did not allow for jazz and its syncopated beat.

It is consequently very dangerous to allow your children to listen to the radio. Be aware to what extent we are drenched with the unfettered lucubrations of Jacques Hélian or Pierre Spiers. That is why I say to you – parents, beware of jazz! Because in addition to the problems already mentioned above, it has been observed that this same jazz music produces violent genetic reaction (pubertas praecox, the Peyronnie Syndrome) in certain individuals. You do not have to look any further for the source of all these maledictions destroying the foundations of contemporary society – creeping club membership, betting on horse races, butterfly catching, *Gone with the Wind*, nicotine poisoning, teenage mothers, the closing of the bordellos, the overture to *William Tell*, grandpa's beard, exorbitant bills, proliferant rectites and anal fistulas, Spartan wheelbarrows, great sportsmen and the Trotskygaullian reaction.

That is why we say to our government – ATTENTION! DANGER! Suppress jazz – halt this embryonic contagion of social rebellion which, without fail, will sooner or later lead to atomic war.

A Useless Programme

(*Jazz News*: November, 1949)

Desiring to help our beloved readers avoid repurchasing issues of this magazine which are repackaged and camouflaged as programmes and come off the press, by chance, just when there happens to be a jazz concert, on the one hand . . .

Considering that the above-mentioned programmes have the same contents no matter what musicians are playing, on the other hand . . .

Considering that the concerts in question unfortunately seem to be increasingly frequent, which is pushing a large number of jazz fans to the brink of bankruptcy . . .

And seeking to abort in its infancy any commercial exploitation of concertgoers by the printed word . . .

Without losing sight of the fact that the listener should be informed of what he might be about to hear, and in order to raise the average level of his general culture without obliging him to learn English, which is after all spoken by 500 million less people than Chinese – the publishers, the editors and the dedicated personnel of *Jazz News* have perfected a prototype programme in which you will find all the repertoire which has been and will be played by all bands past, present and future.

Group A – Concerts Organized by the International Jazz Parade Association

1. Bibope Major
2. Bibope Blues
3. Let's Bebope with (name of leader)
4. Ri-ti-pi-tadle-di-doo
5. Paris Bibope Rebound
6. Tuileries-bope
7. Taxi-bope
8. Muskrat-bope
9. High Society Bope
10. Corned-beef and Jelly Bope
11. Blue 'n' Bebope
12. Ra-da-di-da-bi-bi-oubla-bi
13. . . . Bibope (promoter's name)
14. Saint Louis Bope
15. Body and Soul
16. The Jazz War
17. Dixiebope (a failed collective improvisation)
18. Ablio-Ablio-ou-ou-pabi-pa-ou
19. Solo, by what's his name
20. Intermission
21. Barclay Blues (royalties to Barclay)
22. Cold Blues
23. Blues
24. Relaxing at Camarillo
25. Blues by all

Hip-hip for the good old days (Bugle Call Rag blues, replacing the bridge by five languorous piano chords). Finale and applause.

Group B – Concerts Organized by the Parade Jazz Parade Association

1. New Orleans Major (marching band version)
2. New Orleans, with (name of leader)
3. New Orleans Blues
4. Out of It Blues
5. Parixieland
6. Tuileries Blues
7. Taxi Blues
8. Muskrat Ramble
9. High Society
10. Jam with Champagne Blues

11. Blues in New Orleans
13. Oh, la-la, My Poor Black Heart
15. ... Dixie (first name of the promoter's wife)
17. The Jazz War
19. How Cold It is in the Water, Blues
21. Barclay Blues (royalties to Barclay)
23. Blues
12. ... Dixie (name of promoter)
14. Saint Louis Blues
16. Body and Soul Stomp (boos)
18. Bopsieland (unison line, sloppy)
20. Intermission
22. Hot Blues

24. Finale: As the curtain is lowered, the bandleader appears totally nude carrying his pyjamas. He throws kisses and makes it clear that he is going to bed. General exit under protest.

Did You Know ...

The Olida company accepts no responsibility for the content of this issue.

The war veterans of the eighteenth arrondissement accept no responsibility for the content of this issue.

The Assistant Mayor of Savigny-sur-Orge accepts no responsibility for the content of this issue.

The highway and bridge commissioner, André Ferréol de Lavinière sur Montbard, né Rostopchine, accepts no responsibility for the content of this issue.

M. François Mauriac, of the Académie Française, accepts no responsibility for the content of this issue.

The Happy Children of Nirvana, a dance and fine arts organization, accepts no responsibility for the content of this issue.

Big Ben accepts no responsibility for the content of this issue.

In addition, the following people have asked us to inform the public that at no time have they, even part-time, had anything to do with the editing of this issue of *Jazz News*:

Nephew (Amadeus-Aristotle), personnel director of the eastern urinal network;

Dorigné (Michel), publisher of the *Gazette du Jazz* (a serious paper);

XII (Pius), official Pope

Thorez (Maurice), ex-miner, now major

Gaulle (Charles de), talkative general

Ahmed-Ben-Bougnouf, peanut vendor on the corner of rue de l'Abbaye and rue Saint-Benoit.

So it goes.

ON THE RADIO

(4 November, 1949)

Because this is (I hope) the first in a regular series, let me begin by wishing a good day to my listeners, both ladies and gentlemen.* I am going to speak to you each week about jazz. I realize the subject is a tricky one and that it risks causing hostility and protest. On the other hand, with this subject, like many others, much useless polemic can be avoided if trouble is taken to define the terms to be used.

Radio France is not exempt from a certain amount of valid criticism in this regard – it has much too often pasted a 'jazz' label on products which, no matter how valid they may be in their other lives, have nothing to do with what the majority of critics specializing in the subject consider the real thing. The result is doubly disastrous. Jazz fans consider it fraudulent and stop listening to the radio, while the enemies of jazz use the

---

*In 1949, Radio France asked Boris Vian to speak on jazz once a week. The station introduced the series to its listeners on 4 November with the announcement: 'Starting this week, Boris Vian will explain the art of jazz.' The series ended after thirteen broadcasts, on 28 January, 1950.

This selection is chosen for its general interest and current relevancy, and attempts to avoid duplication of Vian's print articles appearing in this collection.

opportunity to challenge the validity of what they hear which is, in general, some sort of pounding rhythm which has nothing to do with any sort of music whatsoever.

It should be understood that:

1) Jazz is above all the syncopated music of black Americans, from New Orleans Dixieland bands to modernists like Dizzy Gillespie, etcetera.

2) The only valid white jazz is that in which these musicians have mixed the *spirit* of their own (European) ancestors with the black tradition, rather than transposing European forms themselves. The worst examples of such excess are the abominable formations of Paul Whiteman in America and Jack Hylton in England, both of whom were pushed straight to the top in the twenties by racial prejudice and good publicity. Every last one of their recordings is vapid and insincere and has become totally unlistenable today on any level.

3) Attempts by certain critics, incapable of adapting to any sort of change, to discredit the recent evolution of jazz are to be completely ignored except incomprehension and incompetence. All the organic intermediary steps from New Orleans to the contemporary style we seem to be obliged to call 'bebop' (a name I deplore as much as you do) prove it to be obviously just another natural evolution.

That being said, it is evident that with blacks as well as whites, in any style you can mention, evaluation is a matter of careful individual discrimination. One of the principal reproaches with which jazz fans can be confronted is the harm they have done the music they love by abusing superlatives. If 'Soandso is a fantastic musician', OK. But they have cried 'genius' too many times – it must be said here and now that jazz has known very few true geniuses, the most obvious and uncontested of them being Duke Ellington.

This also said, it is, in addition, obvious that there are an enormous number of quality jazz recordings from which any serious listener can discover overwhelming riches. But here, as with anything else of value, initiation is necessary. We will elaborate next week.

How to Recognize Real Jazz

(11 November, 1949)

Last week I tried to establish certain principles that should never be forgotten while listening to jazz. This was to prepare the ground for the first question you will probably ask: 'How can I recognize real jazz when I hear it?'

Many books have been written on the subject. Reading them will give you some idea of the answer. So first I suggest a visit to the library. In the meantime, however, a shortlist of the names of certain musicians will enable you to get started. When you listen to Sidney Bechet, Duke Ellington, Louis Armstrong or Charlie Parker, you can sleep in peace (though this may make listening difficult) − it's real jazz.

On the other hand, Ray Ventura, Yvonne Blanc, Camille Sauvage, Victor Silvester, Guy Lombardo etcetera, produce dance music which might be pleasant and well executed but has nothing in common with jazz other than the melodies and 4/4 time.

It's more complicated than that. Once upon a time Ventura's band included some of the best French jazz musicians. I cite the names at random − Philippe Brun, Combelle, Chaillou, etcetera. But commercial pressures in France, as elsewhere, are such that it is extremely difficult to make a decent living by playing only jazz music . . .

a) because there are not enough good jazz players, which means that, all things considered, the public is not basically wrong to boycott what amounts to a majority of mediocre bands . . .

b) because even if there were, the public would not be large enough. People who have enough money to go out at night want to dance. And it's rare in France that anyone has enough money before that certain age when people begin to prefer unchalleng-ing tangos and safe ballads with their active elements sufficiently castrated so as not to pose any threat on any level.

Without justifying them, this explains why certain nightclub owners, totally lacking any artistic sensibility but with a solid instinct about what brings in customers, prefer the syrupy music of sleepy dance bands to the vigorous tonic of real jazz.

These clubowners are, however, wrong. It is possible to interest the audience in real jazz. The careers of Claude Luter and Jean-Claude Fohrenbach prove it. But we need more young, enthusiastic musicians who are ready to live in near misery while proselytizing. Do not cast the first stone at those who run out of patience; it is not always easy nor even worthwhile to endure misery. You think of your family first.

Which is to say that, all in all, there is not much real jazz to hear in France. Happily, America still exists. There, a growing minority of sincere enthusiasts has, in fact, subsidized French tours by some American musicians. They are also to be thanked for the existence of a small but solid recorded repertoire. This repertoire is what we generally hear over Radio France.

Now that we have got to know one another and that your introduction to theory (unfortunately rather abbreviated) is complete, I intend, during the coming broadcasts, to speak in more detail about the jazz you hear on French radio and jazz in general.

The Listener Can be Excused for not Knowing Coleman Hawkins

(25 November, 1949)

On Monday, 28 November, Paris Inter's 'Jazz Parade' is scheduled to feature Coleman Hawkins, who has just returned to France for the first time in a year and a half. Hawkins will be accompanied by Kenny Clarke, James Moody, Nat Peck, Hubert Fol, Jean-Paul Mengeon and Pierre Michelot – the last three being fine young French musicians.

It is perfectly understandable if my listeners have never heard of Coleman Hawkins. I suppose in a sense one could thank God that he has never been the subject of a gaudy publicity campaign. He has kept his integrity. But it is up to us to inform you about him.

Born in 1904 in Missouri (just like Harry Truman, but any

resemblance ends there), he is black. For years now, he has been unquestionably one of the two greatest masters of the tenor saxophone (the other being Lester Young), a difficult instrument.

It is far too easy to abuse superlatives when it comes to jazz, which tends to bring out the romantic in the listener, but without any doubt Hawkins has affected all the saxophonists who followed, just as Louis Armstrong affected trumpet players.

Since his long stint with Fletcher Henderson's band (1924–34), Coleman Hawkins has been immediately recognizable by his intensely rhythmic eighth- and sixteenth-note passages. He developed a sort of bubbling vehement romanticism which can be described simply as 'inspired'. But most of all, he has always been immediately recognizable by his beautiful tone, his crisp attack and, lately, by profoundly moving serenity and intellectual depth. He is one of those musicians who can be much better understood on record – his true value requires repeated listening to be appreciated. Besides, he's abundantly recorded; we have no complaints.

Physically, Hawkins is of medium height and rather corpulent. When he plays he appears to be totally uninterested in everything and everyone around him including those who are listening to or accompanying him. His style, like his image, makes everything seem so easy, natural and organic that only after he has finished do we realize the extent of the riches he has bestowed on us.

A good number of his recordings are currently on the market and, before the war, Hawkins even recorded in Paris with a formation that included our very own Django Reinhardt, as well as in groups with that other master saxophonist (alto) Benny Carter.

When he recorded 'Body and Soul' on 11 October, 1939, more than ten years ago, it was a kind of revelation. His improvisation based on this beautiful melody was a crystallization of fifteen years' work. His complex assortment of colours enriched the melody with magnificent, elaborate tension which built under perfect control from first to last groove. 'Yesterdays', only recently released in France, is just about as good – only the recording quality is wanting.

So Hawkins is one of those unsung jazz musicians who,

116

without benefit of a publicity machine, creates what must in all objectivity be described as musical masterpieces.

Must a Jazz Critic be a Musician?

(4 December, 1949)

Taking into consideration all the opinions which are hurled at this musician or that band without any risk to the hurler, I wonder how many laymen have asked themselves this question: 'What right does anyone have to assume the title "jazz critic"?' How can anybody pretend to know more than anybody else about a subject which is based on instinct and thus, it would appear, should be understood by any individual with two good ears and an ounce of discrimination?

The question involves arts criticism in general, but I am not presumptuous enough to pose it in its broadest implications, to say nothing of answering. Jazz, however, involves unique particularities, some of which I will now underline.

First of all, jazz is American music, and so the critic is always dependent upon foreign recordings. It is true that there are more concerts here lately but Paris is not yet a city in which it is possible to hear a large assortment of good jazz.

World War II broke off communication with America. This is responsible for the current flap about bop – not many privileged people were able to remain in contact and continue to follow the evolution of black music through the war years. They are in a position to understand that bebop was inevitable, not just some sudden shift. Those of the majority who remained out of touch and assume the contrary are wrong.

Jazz is not free of charge like painting can be, like sculpture and even, by way of libraries, literature. Jazz resembles music in general in this regard. Radio, which can at least provide free recorded music (though you must buy the radio, alas) is much more generous to classical than it is to jazz fans. And the marketplace is better stocked with classical than jazz records. But the most important difference is that jazz is not something fixed like 'Wagner', 'Bach' or 'Mozart'. An improviser must by

117

definition change the repertoire each time he plays it.

Record companies have been making a strong effort recently and there are now more jazz records to choose from in France. But a simple calculation proves that somebody who merely wants to keep up with new releases will, buying twenty records a month, spend close to 70,000 francs a year. Adding the cost of a turntable, needles, etcetera, it is prohibitive for young people, who constitute the principal audience as well as the critics of the future.

Those who do not have enough money to buy all these products can always join an organization like the Hot Club which has a record library for members, though they risk being infected by the sort of maniacs who belong to such clubs. Or they might put themselves at the mercy of collectors. But collectors usually specialize in some style or other and anyway there is a limit to the amount of time you'd want to spend with these people just to hear their recordings.

Nothing but obstacles in the way of our future critics, it seems. Nevertheless, it will be necessary for them to assimilate all the steps of the evolution of jazz. This music grew up at about the same time as such technological developments as recording and the radio. Its audience is growing much faster than that for classical music. The musicians themselves are learning faster, they are relating to each other with more depth of musicianship and feeling all the time. Had radio existed in Mozart's time, his latest work could have been known from one end of Europe to the other the day after he wrote it. Who knows what vocations this would have created, how people in general would have been changed by such fast communication. Jazz critics must be aware if an Armstrong chorus is based on a King Oliver solo. Not that they need to carry a lot of heavy intellectual baggage. A reasonably good ear and memory will suffice.

Here we come back to the oft-disputed point. Must a jazz critic also be a musician? The question never arises when it comes to classical music, where the reverse is more the norm. In jazz it seems that nobody dares express an opinion in public unless they blow into some sort of horn. What a mistake! After all, shouldn't the title's only prerequisite be having published a critique or two? Anyway, nobody cares and it doesn't really matter.

LETTER TO SANTA KLAUS

(*Jazz Hot*: special issue, 1950)

Deer Sanna Claws,

I hope you feel gilty about not packing a rod for Cagney last year so he could put dirty rats who don't dig jazz six octaves under. This year he'll settle for a minor blue piece. And a prescription for *Giter* magazine; he likes to rifle through it.

For Honey in Paris, Texas, camanbare cheeze – and a beeday pleze.

Gnat Hentoff rote you a 5,000-word letter about why he deverves a Learned Father jazz index in his stocking . . . there's a wail of a whole in his discography. Plus too cases of twelve-yeer-old flatted fifths.

Bearendt could use a news editair-in-chaif because he kneeds time to lissen to the sinphonic music of his choosin'. How about a vocalbury for Swerin, and a pair of chops two if you don't mined?

For Vian some foli bergere dancers cause the cat's a saxual maniac and can't get it up to right know more artycals.

Mouldy fig reckerd coalecters need tabs to find their ole el peas.

Layzee jazz fans reqwire fats wallets to pay fur high-buy stearios and all the reishoes.

Don't forget grease for the Bulgians, numbered snow flakes for the Swiss and dikshonerys for the Spanyards beecoz day kant spell. The French wood like seven holydaze a weak.

Plise rememmer Françoise, hooz very innertesting. And Chalklate for everybuddy.

Ur pal,
Chas Band-Fan

Cher pave Noéle

Si t'es onaité, t'as des remorts de pas avoir aporté l'ané dernière un fuzi à Gugusse pour qu'tu tous les grans salingues qui desonore le jaze bande (et i a pas que lui comme dis mon frert qu'a vin tans, moi je ne trouve pas sa drole) alors j'espaire que set ané, tu lui aporte un fuzi à Gugusse et une boite à Camanbaire pour marguerite et des tas d'abonemants pace que sa plait, et mintenant, il fot aussi que je te parle de Charles, il a toujout l'ère osi triste et il fot qu'il trouvent. dent ses soulié un nundexe to Jaze d'orine blaque stone pace qu'i a plein de trouts dans sa diskografie et une groce boite de cantes diminuée et pour Odert, il fot un sou redaqueteur en chaife pace qu'il a pas le tant découté la musique sinfonique de sa prédilèquesion et pour ledru une colone d'ère en zauque embouti et pour Viand une revu des foli bergerent pace que ça mèque la, c'est un obsèdé saxuelle et sa remplasserat sa revut de praisse à ventajeusemant. et pour les colèque- sioneurs de disque il fot des charniaires en papé gomé pour les colé sur des Zalbomes et pour les bailges, il fot du cramique et pour les suces il fot de la nage et pour les Zespamioles, il fot un dicsionère pace que c'est un drol de charabbiat — Et pour les Zamateures de geaze, il fot un portefoye bien guarner paffce que sait fout le nonbre de disquisor anse moman et pis ta nous zaporterat oci la pot du Kent et la consiance trenguil — et oublit pas frensoize pace qu'elle ait treize interecente et des chocolas pour toulmonde.

Joséfe pignerole
amateure de Jaze bande

121

Is There a Moat between Serious Music and Jazz?

(*Radio*: 22 December, 1949)

During discussions about jazz, one of the most frequent questions is if there's an unbridgeable moat between it and 'serious' (what an adjective!) music. Do they have anything in common? Can they be appreciated from two different points of view? Shouldn't one just deal with 'music', period? Is it necessary to line up with the opinionated? (Jazz is the only music, jazz is not music at all, bebop is not jazz, Dixieland is not jazz, and so on.)

Whether we like it or not, certainly in these times of recordings and the radio, all kinds of music influence and connect with each other. You only have to open a magazine and read interviews with musicians to learn that Louis Armstrong loves Guy Lombardo, that Benny Goodman is Barney Bigard's idol, that Charlie Parker's favourite is Paul Hindemith and Debussy charms Duke Ellington. There is only one conclusion to be drawn, and the history of jazz confirms it.

What is at the root of the New Orleans style which can be defined as the first generation of jazz? It is in effect only a more inspiring and easier (because simplified) way of playing the military marches, quadrilles and polkas which were in style during the preceding decades. Everybody knows that the original title of 'Tiger Rag' was 'Praline', and that it was salon music. We know that Alphonse Picou's famous chorus on 'High Society', practised by several generations of clarinettists, is a copy of the piccolo part of a famous march. At least a thousand examples prove that such thematic influences abound.

On the other hand, to pretend that jazz is a European invention is going too far. Because thematic influence, considerable though it may be, constitutes only one small element in its personality. What is essential and fascinating is the collision, thanks to the blacks, between different traditions and an everyday, banal event like the signpainter who sings the song, 'deforming' it, which he hears on the radio.

So we find in effect that, in the case of the blacks, the deformation turns into a transformation, that the deformed object becomes superior to the original because of the contribution of energy and personality it did not have at the beginning. I cannot deny that this contribution can be negative. Which is to say that in certain cases the transformation of ancestral folklore might deform it. Some experts use this argument to come to a reactionary conclusion which assigns the definition 'authentic' only to jazz based on old-time blues and work songs – they deny, for example, any value to the influence of Tin Pan Alley, which, I believe, goes too far and eliminates too much essential material.

Others go to the other extreme, holding that the modern style called bebop is nothing but a simplified, vulgar parody of contemporary 'serious' composers like Stravinsky and Milhaud – even Schoenberg (they have not as yet spoken much of Bartók, but, patience, they will).

Some dig moats, others see only plains.

The truth is that the harmonic vocabulary of jazz grows larger every day – like every living music it gets richer as it evolves. The spirit of jazz has not changed – inflexion, timbre. Everything that was there remains – 'drive', 'swing', all those words which defy definition are just as essential for jazzmen today as yesterday.

Conclusion? Is there a moat? Of course! It is easy to jump over. There's music on both sides.

Papal Decrees

(*Jazz Hot*: special edition, 1950)

A collective improvisation on sacred themes by M. Panassié, otherwise known under the critical name of Our Holy Father Hugues I, Pope of Jazz.

O Holy and Venerable Pontiff:

We are pained by the general sentence of excommunication as published in your Clinker of last 1 November. Although we are aware of our profound unworthiness, we did not think the devil had impregnated us humble folk with enough impurity to awaken the formidable wrath with which you pummel heretical Worms.

Terrified by the imminent menace of punishment by the Gods, from which only the well-known forgiving nature of Your Holiness can save us, and searching for The Way back to more orthodox beliefs, we humbly and fervently kneel before the Bright Emanations of Your Mind in order to be taught the Dogma of True Jazz which you have tried so hard to spread over the ages in *La Revue du Jazz*, *Le Bulletin du Hot Club de France* and other magazines, daily and otherwise and, also alas, through the nauseating channel of this monthly paper (the number of

124

readers of which have been declining over the past three years, as you yourself have said) titled *Jazzote* of which you were the Guru until the time of the Great Schism, when the poisonous tentacles of bebop spread disharmony and dissonance across the land.

We have laboured hard and long poring over the texts which you have written in Bold Letters. We have taken the liberty to probe into the archives of *Jazz Hot* (1934) way back before the deluge, to the times when 'the structures of Johnny Dodds's phrasing were vulgar' (p. 128), Teschemacher was enthroned as '100 times better than all other clarinettists, black or white' (p. 128), and Jimmie Noone revealed 'an ugly texture and bleating sonority' (p. 124). It is good that the nine-headed Bebopian monster had not yet been born. However, the example of Lester Young, who, in 1944 often played 'over-elaborated phrases and squeezed a sound reminiscent of an automobile horn out of his saxophone' (*Les Rois de Jazz*, p. 189) should have warned us about the coming demonic scourge that would desecrate the Sacred Texts until the Holy Year of your Triumph over Evil: 1947.

We now know that the last have become the first, that Jimmy and Johnny are the true giants, that 'nothing in this world should stop you from hearing Lester's magnificent solo' (*La Revue du Jazz*, February, 1949), and that a camel will pass through the eye of a needle with greater ease than Teschemacher will earn praise from Your Holiness.

And so here is the essential of your Gospel which we endeavour, with true humility, to clarify. The following colloquium is for the benefit of all sinners who refuse to give up hope of salvation.

Catechism of the Holy Father Hugues Premier

QUESTION: What is bebop?
  ANSWER: It is the newest form of jazz (*La Bataille*, 30.7.47).
  Q: Can bebop really be called jazz?
  A: Saxophonist Charlie Parker, trumpeter Howard McGhee

125

and pianist Bud Powell often know how to make first-class jazz in this new framework (*Paris Presse* 22.2.48).

Q: When was bebop born?

A: Bebop was born in 1940, when Charlie Parker recorded superb solos on Decca with Jay McShann's fine band. His style was simpler than it is today, but it was excellent (*Bulletin Panassié*, no. 3, October, 1947).

Q: Should we be against bebop?

A: Delaunay employs arguments against me worthy of a political campaign, he tries to pass me off as an enemy of bebop. I am not an enemy of any style (ibid).

Q: Should we try to promote the popularity of bebop?

A: Today I address a solemn appeal to all the Hot Clubs. I affirm that any HC which persists in promoting bebop should be excluded from our Federation (*La Revue du Jazz*, November, 1949).

Q: So what should we think of bebop?

A: It's a perfectly legitimate and from many points of view interesting evolution in jazz (*Bulletin Panassié*, October, 1947).

Q: What else can you tell us?

A: Bebop rejects essential elements of the black tradition (*Revue du Jazz*, October, 1949).

Q: Specifically, how can this style be criticized?

A: In the widest sense, bebop cannot be criticized. It is absolutely logical. From the rhythmical point of view, it introduced a new pulse into jazz, a pulse which we first perceived in certain arrangements by bands such as Count Basie's and in soloists like Lionel Hampton (*Bulletin Panassié*, no. 3, October, 1947).

Q: Exactly what is bebop?

A: Bebop is nothing but one big mistake (Louis Armstrong, quoted by His Holiness in the *Revue du Jazz*, October, 1949).

Q: But what is the personal opinion of Your Holiness?

A: This is what I think about bebop. A perfectly legitimate evolution, interesting from many points of view (*Bulletin Panassié*, no. 3, October, 1947).

Q: What advice does Your Holiness have for jazz fans?

A: The fans should immediately stop listening to bebop, which wears out the ears and leads to decreasing sensitivity and a general loss of enthusiasm (*Revue du Jazz*, October, 1949).

Q: How worthwhile is bebop?

A: Like any other style, like all music, bebop is only as worthwhile as the musicians who create and interpret it (liner notes for a Don Byas album).

Q: How worthwhile are the musicians who create and interpret it?

A: We are not stupid enough to suggest that all boppers are bad musicians. On the contrary, we believe that people like Charlie Parker, Thelonious Monk, Bud Powell, J.J. Johnson, Gillespie, Howard McGhee, Fats Navarro, Miles Davis, Kenny Clarke and Max Roach are very talented. We only say that they are moving in a direction away from real jazz (*Revue du Jazz*, October, 1949).

Q: So bebop is not real jazz?

A: Charlie Parker, Howard McGhee and Bud Powell have often played first-class jazz in the new style (*Paris Presse*, 22.2.48).

Q: So bebop is in fact real jazz?

A: Anybody can of course be interested as much as they like in bebop, only in that case they should not pretend to be supporters of real jazz (*Revue du Jazz*, October, 1949).

Q: What has bebop contributed?

A: This new style is remarkable for its variety and rhythmic unpredictability. Harmonically, these musicians continually stray from the traditional tonality of the songs on which they improvise. This process can neither be praised nor criticized per se, it is only as worthwhile as the musicians who do it (*Paris Presse*, 22.2.48).

Q: Is bebop decadent?

A: Jazz is a music which is constantly renewing itself; it is very much alive despite the pessimistic predictions of some troubled souls (ibid).

Q: What will happen to people who listen to bebop?

A: They will become disgusted with music, and with life (*Revue du Jazz*, October, 1949).

Q: Should we be tolerant of them?

A: It would be good to put aside all of these internecine disputes between fans of old and modern styles. But I am not asking anybody to force anybody else to listen to records they do not enjoy – no matter how desirable the opening of new horizons might be. I would just like people to stop condemning any form of jazz in which they personally do not hear beauty (*Jazz Hot*, no. 9, October, 1949).

Q: May we play bebop, or in any case listen to it?

A: I understand that some people, under the pretext of having a 'tolerant' nature, permit the boppers to occupy a place in jazz history . . . Reading or listening to such ideas, the uninitiated will unfortunately become accustomed to considering bop as the real thing (*Revue du Jazz*, November, 1949).

Q: Is bop jazz?

A: It's the newest form of jazz (*La Bataille*, 30.7.47).

Q: What should be said to people who do not like bebop?

A: I do not wish to force anybody to listen only to old New Orleans jazz records, as good as they may be. I only want to tell these people that by not listening to contemporary jazz carefully and studying it closely they are depriving themselves of enormous musical pleasure (*Jazz Hot*, October, 1946).

Q: What do musicians think of bebop?

A: (Exegetic note: the surest way to Truth here is to refer to American magazines. Several musicians blessed by the Holy Father are, in fact, anti-bebop.)

Q: How much importance should be accorded to musicians' opinions?

A: We should certainly be influenced by the opinions of some musicians, but this can be arbitrary because nothing proves that these particular musicians are thinking in the right way (*Jazz Hot*, April, 1946).

Q: (Exegetic note: the utilization of these ancient [1946] pronouncements can be dangerous, they run the danger of being pronounced blasphemous.)

Q: Should one be against bebop a priori?

A: We are not against bebop a priori. Like Benny Carter, we love it so long as it swings and they play melodies (*Bulletin du HCF*, no. 3, May–June, 1948).

Q: Is it permitted to change our point of view?

A: Changing your point of view is permitted. But if the change is sincere it will come imperceptibly and you should not hide it like something shameful (*Revue du Jazz*, November, 1949).

Q: Can bebop be danced to?

A: This style is distinguished above all by the continual

contrast between the traditional 4/4 time of jazz and stop-time rhythms reminiscent of the steps of the great black American dancers (liner notes, Byas album).

Q: Have bop bands played in black dancehalls?

A: The Savoy in Harlem tried hiring bop bands one or two times. The effect was disastrous: not a dancer remained on the floor (*Revue du Jazz*, October, 1949).

Q: Why are there no dancers for the bebop bands?

A: Black people feel like dancing only to a swinging rhythm section (*Revue du Jazz*, October, 1949).

Q: So bop doesn't swing?

A: With 'Bird's Nest' and 'Cool Blues', Charlie Parker gives a good demonstration of bop. There are many surprises and the swing is considerable (*Bulletin du HCF*, March/April, 1948).

Q: Isn't Charlie Parker a bebop musician?

A: He is one of its creators (*La Revue du Jazz*, February, 1949).

Q: Does he swing?

A: He has a lot of ideas and he swings (ibid).

Q: What should we think about Howard McGhee's bop sextet?

A: I prefer this band's ensemble playing, which is executed with lots of swing. Most of all I like Charlie Parker's interpretation of the arrangement of 'Indiana', which is extremely danceable (*Bulletin du HCF*, no. 3, May/June, 1948).

Q: What should we think about Gillespie?

A: Gramaphone just released two sides of Gillespie's big band . . . The ensembles have punch and they swing, though not as hard as they could (ibid).

Q: Does bebop swing at all?

A: Bop is moving away from the jazz tradition . . . it is neglecting the element of swing (*La Revue du Jazz*, October, 1949).

Q: What should we think about Miles Davis?

A: An extremely talented trumpet player who has the potential to be a jazz great (*La Revue du Jazz*, April, 1949).

Q: What else should we think about Parker?

A: It's not unimportant that Parker played with Jay McShann's blues band; he learned to utilize the eternal roots of jazz (*Revue du Jazz*, June/July, 1949).

129

Q: Is he King of Jazz?

A: (Exegetic note: Hugues I does not answer that question specifically, but he published an article about Parker under the general title 'King of Jazz' in issue no. 2 of *La Revue du Jazz*. One would thus be safe in saying that Parker is a King of Jazz.)

Q: What else should we think about Gillespie?

A: Gillespie is a talented musician (*Bulletin Panassié*, no. 3, October, 1947).

Q: Is it possible to say that Louis Armstrong is more talented than Gillespie?

A: Anybody who mentions Gillespie's name in the same sentence as Louis Armstrong is ignorant (*Revue du Jazz*, October, 1949).

Q: Should we attack bebop?

A: Those who preach bebop are reactionaries (ibid).

Q: Should we attack bebop?

A: Delaunay obviously lacks imagination because he keeps riding the same old warhorse pretending to believe that I attack rebop (*Bulletin du HCF*, no. 1, 1947).

Conclusion

Permeated with Fervour as we are, we trust that our analysis of The Texts have penetrated The Essence of the Sacred Verbs of His Holiness. Without forgetting that we False Prophets of Jazz are prone to error, we think we have herein summarized the essential of the Words of the Holy Father. (What's one decree more or less?)

Bebop is not jazz, rebop is. As far as bop by itself is concerned, the question remains controversial and will no doubt be resolved only by calling an Ecumenical Council to resolve this gordian knot which might otherwise distort the delicate tissue of Faith.

Charlie Parker is a great musician but his music is detestable. Gillespie has talent, but what's so great about talent? As for the Holy Father, he is tolerance personified. But if you have the misfortune to play a flatted fifth on your ophicleide, even if you borrowed it from King Oliver's cousin, you appear to have every chance to rot in Hell for Eternity.

And so we deduce from the above, after consulting with four experts in Canonical Law, that all evidence points to the fact that once more Hugues I has not erred.

(signed)
The False Prophets of Jazz
Charles Delaunay
André Hodeir
Boris Vian

JAZZ ON STAGE

(Radio, 5 January, 1950)

Issue no. 5 of *Gazette du Jazz*, a small newsletter in which one can, between monumental nonsense, read some interesting articles and which has the additional value of enlarging the market for jazz critics, has just published a 'paper' by Georges Baume dealing with 'Jazz Parade', name of the weekly concert series in the Edouard VII theatre as well as a Monday-night show on Radio France. Georges Baume is well-known to listeners as the host of this programme, one of the most lively and eclectic jazz shows, which also broadcasts recordings of their live concerts.

The perspective here involves, on the one hand, a reflection on the nature of jazz in a concert hall in general and on the value and implications of an organization like Jazz Parade on the other.

The question has often been posed. Does presenting jazz on a concert stage inhibit its improvisational soul – cool off, as it were, its existential heat? An immobile and attentive audience lined up in seats does not encourage the taking of risks. Exhibitionism is encouraged, as are tried and true show-business tricks. On the contrary, watching people dance, it would seem, excites musicians to go all out, as does the 'swinging' atmosphere of a club in general.

I am perfectly willing to agree with either opinion. Either argument might be just as strong. It all depends on the conjuncture of the musicians and the circumstances.

I've already said here that most clubs tend to cater to a rich clientele. These sort of people want to be able to dance, and most of them are no longer youngsters. Like Armstrong recently recalled in the American jazz magazine *Metronome*: 'We are playing for old people; after all, they are the ones with the money.'

But let's take it one step further – when we take our girlfriend out dancing it's to be with her not to listen to the band. So a band without too much personality which leaves us free to try and touch the heart of our baby is better fitted to the occasion. Otherwise we might be tempted to look at the bandstand and stop in the middle of a sweet little nothing to hear the trumpet solo, which she would find, quite understandably, rather annoying.

In order to have its true value, then, it may be necessary for jazz to climb on stage and run the corresponding risks, the greatest being loss of sincerity. But then the stage also presents certain advantages.

So long as the theatre involved is designed with a minimum amount of ambience – and in this sense, the Edouard VII, which is not too large, seems much better adapted to jazz than Pleyel or Chaillot – playing on stage requires more serious rehearsing and better instrumental technique. The attention of the audience is more focused. Stages are much more exigent than dancehalls or some cave in Saint Germain. A mistake which might get by in a jam-session atmosphere would make a concert-hall audience cringe.

The essential element here is a correct balance between arrangements and improvisation, a balance arrived at by the greatest and purest jazz names like Jelly Roll Morton, King Oliver, Basie and Gillespie.

And so the greatest contribution of the Jazz Parade organization has been to force young musicians to cultivate elements which

133

they often otherwise neglect: clean execution and co-ordination.

In our next programme we will try to see if Jazz Parade has realized all of its ambitions.

More Reflections on Jazz on the Radio

(12 January, 1950)

Has Jazz Parade realized all its objectives as defined at the beginning by Georges Baume's slogan: 'Jazz Concerts à la Lamoureux'?*

It remains to be seen.

Is it realistic to hope for a jazz equivalent to the rehearsed, disciplined, repertory orchestra which performed under Lamoureux?

In fact at the very beginning, Jazz Parade should have created a big band by recruiting musicians for whom playing jazz is more than just making a living, auditioning them with similar criteria as symphony orchestras, and then hiring a talented, experienced and respected young leader, for which there are several qualified candidates in France.

The greatest difficulty for a white big band is to play an arrangement with the right feeling without the advantage of having lived the black tradition. Coloured musicians are able to play written notes with as much fiery 'swing' as when they improvise. Let's not forget the fact that classical musicians are automatic inheritors of a musical culture and tradition at least four centuries old. Jazz, on the other hand, which is effortlessly felt and expressed by a black musician, cannot be assimilated by a white person without a continuous effort of conscious will, which generally does not show any results for a very long time.

That is why we have said many times, including on this programme, that 'symphonic jazz' cannot be taken seriously by anyone who appreciates real jazz. Because there are, on the one hand, nothing but arrangements, and on the other its feeling,

---

*Nineteenth-century violinist and conductor who inaugurated a popular series of classical concerts.

with very few exceptions, never refers to the culture and spirit of jazz.

A jazz musician does not put an arrangement 'in place' in the same manner as a classical musician. His attack, inflection and technique differ sometimes from day to day. It is mere coincidence that certain bebop trumpet players sound 'classical'. As critic Lucien Malson reminds us in the *Jazz Hot* of December, 1949:

> One day in my house, I played some bebop records for a well-known organist who is not versed in jazz. I asked him what the difference was between jazz and classical instrumentalists. He said that he believed it was first of all a matter of execution – the way the notes are attacked, the articulation of the phrases and the concept of intonation, the way a jazz musician will arrive at a note from a quarter tone up or down. But mostly a jazz player is recognizable by the warmth of his sound.

French jazz musicians are well enough aware of all that and there are definitely enough of them who are capable of playing in the idiom to form a band that could serve as a 'Lamoureux Orchestra' for Jazz Parade. Not only would it be a pleasure to hear them every week, such a formation would also bear witness to the evolution and we hope progress of jazz on stage.*

This enterprise involves a number of risks. Soloists must be free to develop their inspiration. We must constantly remember the essential element – loose execution – even on slow tempos on which warmth is all too often replaced by syrup. The repertoire must be renewed, new arrangers hired. There must be good team spirit. And the black psyche must be the model, as always with jazz.

This being said, we know what elements to look for. Well now, Jazz Parade. Bravo so far. What next?

---

*Translator's note: A subsidized 'Orchestre National de Jazz' was formed under the auspices of the Ministry of Culture in 1986.

COLEMAN HAWKINS/HOWARD MCGHEE SEXTET

Record Review: 'April in Paris'; 'Stardust'.

Sir Charles Thompson (p), Allan Reuss (g), Pettiford (b), and Denzil Best (d) support this record's co-leaders. After a nice exposition by Hawkins, McGhee, who seems to be out of tune with everybody else, takes a not very inspired chorus. The 'chug chug' of Reuss's guitar does not sound as if it belongs here. Without being really terrible, this record suffers when compared to Charlie Parker's 'April in Paris' – that devil Zebird has got us used to a lot more intelligent stuff than Hawkins can play, he makes the latter sound superficial. McGhee introduces 'Stardust', Hawk takes care of the middle . . . no, decidedly that totally misses the point . . . this entire thing is like rereading Lamartine after Kafka. The fact is, I would have liked it ten years ago. I am hearing it too late.

SENSATIONAL COCKTAILS

(*Jazz News*: March, 1950)

I've been editor for two months already! How time flies when you're having fun. During that period, I discovered a recipe for a really sensational cocktail – pour a glass of Cointreau, a glass of lemon-juice liqueur, a glass of kirsch, add sugar and ice in a beaker and shake well. Pour into a beer mug and then add dry, chilled champagne to the brim. You can drink this like lemonade; it helps pass the time. But let's get to the point. Our previous issue has earned nothing but reproaches. That being said, everybody agrees about one thing. There were no girlie photos. Well, it was conscious – we were saving them for this issue.

As you might imagine, finding enough women to fill this issue was something of a tour-de-force. Which accounts for its late publication. (This is supposed to be funny, but we need some justification for the scandalous inertia of those responsible for the delay.) In return for your patience, I recommend the following – take a bottle of vodka, crème de cacao and Cointreau and mix 3/4ths of the first with 1/8th of each of the two others in an ice-filled beaker. If you have taken the trouble to choose a fifty-seven-degree vodka, the effect will be immediate – and will not harm your liver. For added body, place on your turntable an

MGM platter written by Sy Oliver titled 'Slow Burn'. Which is, by the way, the name of this swinging cocktail.

Perhaps, you may be saying to yourself, perhaps he is handing out these chemical formulas to dull our perceptions, because he is depressed, just to fill the page, or because he's drunk. Well, no, my cherished readers, it is not by chance that this editorial already includes two practical recipes. Because it is our intention to make this classy review a didactic magazine to help raise the intellectual level of jazz fans, who may never be smart enough to understand the depth and beauty of the twelve pages of intelligent analytical articles which we dump on the market every month, and who will continue to run not walk to throw it into the nearest rubbish bin.

Yes, *Jazz News* has chosen the most difficult road (if nothing else, we have guts – *Jazz News* is owned, among other things, by Eddie Barclay, the biggest crook since the beginning of time), the apostolate road. We persist, and will continue to persist, as long as this review, burdened with idiotic writers, manages to avoid bankruptcy, to try and make you, valued readers, the most elite of all jazz fans and even, putting it mildly, the most elite of all Frenchmen. Do you realize the importance of your mission? Think of your future role if, God willing, we succeed. Frenchmen, the moment has arrived. Take a shaker, fill it with 1/3rd cognac, 1/3rd crème-de-fraise Héritier-Guyot, 1/3rd whipped cream, shake well and serve in a cocktail glass. It's called 'Rosemilk', and is good for your health.

THE ART OF DIMINISHED FIFTHS

(*Jazz News*: March, 1950)

Now that everybody is talking about it, we thought it would be a good idea to bring our readers up to date about a new art people are bad-mouthing a lot lately: bebop. After studying textbooks by the only reliable scource, M. Hugues Panassié, we have come to the conclusion that bebop is essentially the art of diminished fifths. Our collaborator Eddy Barnard, known as Eddy-the-Barbarian, insisted on writing down his thoughts on the subject and we undertook to translate them because he mutilates the French language with outrageous disrespect.

1) A primitive method consists of amputating one end of the fifth. This practice can be traced back to the emperor Charles the Fifth, whom we salute as the precursor of bop.

2) A more brutal amputation was practised by the Stammerers in northern France – the Fi-fil-filth-fifth method.

3) The classic diminishing method of our grandmothers – drop a stitch every two or three rows. This is called 'Knitty-gritty'.

4) Issue confidential buy-orders for a large block of fifths and then dump them all on the market without warning. The fifth will diminish automatically by the law of supply and demand. The diminished stockbroker method.

5) Large doses of detergent poured into a family-size washing-machine will result in massive quantities of diminished fifths. The housewife method, also known as 'The Clean Shrink'.

6) Take an acclaimed musician and hire him, under the pretext of demonstrating correct French pronunciation, to repeat the following phrase out loud: 'The fifth is an anti-jazz interval which Buddy Bolden disapproved of.' Record it on tape and publish the text in your official organ. Great orchestrators call this method 'Diminishing by Prestige'.

7) Play your records on a turntable using an expensive diamond stylus. Already diminished fifths will eventually evaporate, and everything else will diminish considerably in thickness and intensity. The oldest rag will sound boppish – 'Diminishing by Perfection'.

8) Buy codeine syrup in your neighbourhood pharmacy.

Some Recommendations

9) We sound a warning note for those who have the idea to play howel, mortice knife or woodworking plane – instruments which demand precision and fast fingering which will always remain the exclusive property of superior soloists. Superior bop soloists (names furnished upon request) have spoken to us of their aversion to those who use the plane without proper preparation and consequently do considerable damage to real jazz music.

10) Above all, never confuse a diminished fifth with an augmented fourth because Mme. Nadia Boulanger has a weak heart.

11–12) Nothing to do with anything . . . we had to fill out the page.

Why We Detest Jazz (1)

. . . Investigative reporting for *Jazz News* by Freddy Flabby: (Saturday painter, winner of the Agricultural 'Grand-Croix du Mérite', colonial doctor and ex-male nurse)

(*Jazz News*: March, 1950)

The article 'Jazz is Dangerous' in our last issue warned you about the serious physical problems which can come from jazz-abuse. Hoping to enlarge the debate, we have decided to reserve one page for the enemies of jazz, who heretofore have not had any journalistic platform. This injustice will now be corrected, and we hope that everybody who is, as we are, profoundly disgusted by jazz will make it their duty to send our editors material for the new page. We particularly welcome articles that investigate the hypocritical lie at the root of this rotten corpse, because objective reasoning leads inevitably to rejection of that jungle music called jazz, which is obviously unworthy of any white man who drinks pernod, drives a limousine and feels up his best friend's wife while dancing the

141

samba. We welcome, with particular enthusiasm, calumnies, gossip and slander calculated to ruin the reputations of big-name jazz musicians, as well as elegiac prose about individuals who heap dishonour upon what our enemies call 'real jazz'.

There will be no censorship – if we read in *Paris-Match* that Louis Armstrong wears flowered underwear and that he loves brightly coloured handkerchiefs, we will reproduce the information in integral form, and so much the better if it isn't true. Down with jazz, that degenerate music – long live our very own military marches, the bourgeoisie and so on.

Among the material already received, we cite in particular an anonymous envelope containing a remarkable study entitled 'Jazz and Epiphany'. This document is an admirable indictment of jazz, written in clear and simple language, and the harm such articles can do to that banal music cannot be overestimated.

Our most sincere compliments to the fine Parisian weekly magazine, *La Presse*, several lines from which we cannot resist the pleasure of citing. After correctly deploring the loss of the first 'racktimes' (*sic*) which inspired the pioneers of jazz, *La Presse* deals with recent declarations by Armstrong concerning bebop. The thrust is something like this . . .

The playing of Armstrong and his celebrated pianist Earl Hines, exponents of the New Orleans style, were not enough to overcome the 'bellowing bebop of Russell Moore' (known as Big Chief).

Upon arriving in Paris, Louis Armstrong had not hesitated to call bebop 'wrestling music'. Maybe that's why *La Presse* mentioned Big Chief, who is *big*. Well, I certainly hope their fine critique will make the poorly informed very, very angry. Bravo, *La Presse*! We support you all the way.

We are trying to procure sexy photos of bad female singers who lure into their insidiously charming traps those imbeciles who still prefer the vulgarity of someone like Bessie Smith to the sweet, captivating voices of Martha Tilton or Anita O'Day.

Dr F. Flabby

THE PERFECT CRITIC ... DREAM OR REALITY?

(*Jazz News*: March, 1950)

Critics rarely talk about a jazz musician without indicting him for having been influenced by Célestin Bandichou while bottle-feeding, by 'Rex' Doublezap when pubescent and, later, by the legendary Jonathan Ferguson Brother. Rarely indeed, and easy to understand why.

In-depth analysis of any given artist involves taking pains to write something more profound than mere comparisons. This is obviously much more tiring work.

We might ask ourselves if it is even possible to find one musician who has totally original ideas, sound, phrasing, attack, inflexion, or any of the attributes that would constitute the dream improviser. We could possibly cite Johnny Hodges, Stuff Smith, Harry Carney, Art Tatum ... I am sure that even this shortlist could be the subject of many arguments. But with everybody else, your run-of-the-mill jazz critic would content himself with admiring the maturity of whom Whoozis based his playing on ten years ago.

Antecedents are without doubt meaningful – but why stop with one generation? I firmly believe that Duke Ellington, Hines and others plagiarized Chopin, because after all, they all play the same eighty-eight keys on the piano.

Nevertheless, when two researchers who are not in communication in two different countries invent similar machines at about the same time (this happened with the phonograph, the telephone, etcetera), does anyone accuse them of having copied from each other?

No, it is just 'something that was in the air'.

If you look hard enough, you can always find the germ of any idea in the work of someone else. The words that we use, weren't they also invented by someone else? For my part, I find it more interesting to try and analyse wider influences, because then the conclusions are deeper and you can get closer to the heart of the matter. It is meritorious for a musician to develop, to perfect something a predecessor could – perhaps unconsciously – only hint at. Influence may be important, but only influence assimilated as raw material to be developed through further searching, and it isn't really very relevant to our judgement of the completed work in any case.

Critics exaggerate the implications of stylistic influence (it's convenient; you can also write a series of articles titled . . . 'Two Great Drummers', 'Three Great Trumpeters', 'Four Great Tenormen', etcetera) to the point of bemoaning the influence of Coleman Hawkins on Lester Young, who might just possibly have played like Hawkins had Hawkins never existed.

Maybe that's going a bit far, but it is necessary to take logic to its (illogical) extreme if you want to refute its stupidity (which can also be turned against you just when you think you've won).

These reflections bring us to our (logical) conclusion. Instead of classifying a musician by comparing him to another musician – more or less known to the reader, who may or may not be interested in him – the critic should describe him objectively, in context, using contemporary values as far as possible. The musician should be situated within his own epoch clearly enough to define the sources. We do not ignore the influence of King Oliver on Louis – but the style of the latter is perhaps just as much a result of his taste for the Hot Potatoes or the music of Guy Lombardo, which could be the subject of a stylistic study that might teach us more than the endless genealogical laundry lists jazz critics have so far been offering us.

Michel Delaroche

144

WOMEN AND JAZZ

(*Jazz News*: March, 1950)

If people listening to the recordings of Savannah Churchill (Blue Star) might for a moment suspect they are hearing a man's voice, we trust that the accompanying photograph will correct their error – as well as provide them with some welcome joie de vivre. Savannah Churchill is not a great singing 'star', to use the common expression, but she must have more than an ordinary amount of talent because she sang on several records with Benny Carter. As far as biographical details are concerned, we have none at our disposal. We could make them up, of course, but there isn't enough room here anyway. Too bad – maybe next time.

Sarah Vaughan is a young singer in the modern vein who became famous by working hard and learning her trade. Her style is very complex, slightly strained perhaps, but not at all disagreeable. She specializes in difficult intervals and an inventive approach to melody which is very much appreciated by bop musicians – you know, those miserable little bastards who pass their time bleating into their horns on stage when they are not leaving it in the middle of a tune to go to the men's room. But her appeal is obviously also wider because older musicians like Earl Hines have hired her to sing with them.

Dinah Washington has a rather braying voice, but you can't see it in the photo printed on the following page, and we have to admit that her voice subtracts nothing from her sex appeal. If the photo is true to life, it would take some self-control to keep your hands off her. Dinah Washington has made quite a few fine records. The Keynote label in particular has released four sides on which her accompanist, the pianist Milt Buckner, is particularly impressive. Dinah Washington's legs are also particularly impressive. They allow her to move around as though she were just another ordinary person, which does not, looking at the rest of her, seem to be the case. Very strange.

Why We Detest Jazz (2)

. . . Another in our series of articles by the talented Dr Freddy Flabby: (Tuesday painter, Grand Master in the Persian Order of the Green Dog, licensed pharmacist and diaper-changer in the Bastille Maternity Ward)

(*Jazz News*: April, 1950)

It is with great enthusiasm that I salute the hassole* named Jean Guitton who has delivered a mortal blow to jazz in an issue of *Images Musicales*, a classical-music publication consecrated to the same noble task I undertake here. Vive Jean Guitton, king of all hassoles, and vive *Images Musicales*, which had the intelligence to acquire the invaluable collaboration of this talented fellow. I feel it my duty to reproduce the entire conclusion of his research, bursting with sincerity and understanding, and so making it clear to what point Jean Guitton has succeeded in breaking through to the essence of jazz music which – we can

---

*The highest rank of Tibetan lamas. Also written 'hawsoule'.

never stress it often enough – has done incalculable harm to our civilization – without it, we would never have known the hydrogen bomb, Chinese Communists, Chopin (precursor of jazz, according to Guitton) and all the other abominations of modern civilization including our glandular degeneration as a result of the promiscuous consummation of the sexual act. This hassole of hassoles, Guitton, to whom we award our 'Antijaz-zeur' medal of the year, explains this with lucidity . . .

Jazz destroys all noble artistic sensibilities because it 'frees our consciousness from the detestable uncreative routine' (to use the words of one of our correspondents) we have inherited from our venerated masters . . . [Note by Dr F. Flabby: Jean Guitton is referring to the point of view of a young worshipper of this diabolical music, and his venerated prose is in reaction to that cowardly attack.]

. . . Ignorance of what actually constitutes technique would be the only excuse for praise of the 'impressive virtuosity' of these so-called musicians . . . It must be emphasized that students who, guided by consummate masters, practise intensely for six hours a day, become virtuosos only after fifteen to twenty years of study – and that, on the other hand, some high-school student who begins to toy around with one instrument or another is consecrated as a jazz idol by the age of nineteen.

As for the visual impression of these talented individuals, we must apologize for not appreciating their constant hysterical and tiresome twitches which are equalled only by the depression the sight of them plunges us into . . . [Note by Dr F. Flabby: I was the first one to denounce the physiological problems jazz has engendered and I am proud to acknowledge Jean Guitton as my favourite disciple, as well as his point of view, which plunges us into anything but vague depression. With what supreme ease he manipulates the language . . . What daring!]

. . . From that point, it is only one small quick step to understand how jazz deforms the artistic sensibility, and to learn a lesson from it.

They claim to be renewing the art of music by developing an embryonic form of folklore, which in fact does not exist except for tom-toms in the jungle. This is the equivalent of a professor asking for lessons from a student he has just taught. Everything the Negroes have discovered in music comes from imitating European folklore in their manner after contact with our civilization . . . [Note by Dr F. Flabby: We recognize, in passing, the positive influence of M. Coeuroy, the champion pre-Guitton Antijazzeur, who was the first to reveal to the world, during the Occupation in 1943, that, far from being 'Negroid', jazz originated in Europe.]

. . . And we interpret this development as a big step backwards rather than a forward-looking revolution. Negroes are perhaps the only race not to possess any folk traditions, in the strict sense of the word. If you know of one, please inform us. Their dances or pantomimes are nothing but a spectacular manner of expressing and communicating a form of excitement which serves only to provoke eroticism.

. . . Europeans should not glorify such primitive source-material while so many black students in our universities try so hard to understand the inexhaustible qualities contained in the works of our great European classical masters.

You see, my dear readers, when you are named Freddy Flabby, you are proud to quote a Jean Guitton.

Dr F. Flabby

Festival of Laughs

by Andy Blackchic

(*Jazz News*: April, 1950)

The congenial Hot Club of the sixteenth arrondissement took the bull by the horns by deciding to spread the good word among the heathen, and even the holy, by organizing a mini-jazz festival at the Ranelagh Theatre.

They had signed one star: Buck Clayton, the pièce de résistance.

The first half featured the elegant Steffy and Kentucky orchestras. The former is an advanced, if not bebop, jazz band led by the unforgettable voice and mannerisms of the immortal Harry Fox. Followed by the Kentucky band. The first half was thus honestly billed. You knew what to expect.

Which leaves Buck Clayton. Deciding whom to get to accompany him, they did not look very far – the very Parisian Bernard Amouroux, Buddy Jones to his friends, and his dynamic formation were all close by. Amouroux, a dynamic businessman, organized everything, took care of his leader's responsibility with acumen, fitted a new reed on the mouthpiece

150

of his saxophone, and 'got into it', as he likes to say.

Buck Clayton had to call up all his resources to make it to the end. It would serve no purpose to single out each of Buddy Jones's 'musicians'. The fearless discords and lack of swing with which they flooded the hall made the audience laugh. A joker who brought along a car horn was disappointed to be almost totally ignored; most of the audience thought the honks were coming from the stage. We breathed a little easier when Buck soloed with the rhythm section, but this was only on one or two tunes.

The circus ended when the hall was half empty and the Amouroussiens gave up the good fight.

They kept refusing to solo, deferring to their colleagues, much to the amusement of the public, and finally nobody on the stage was willing to take responsibility for the next solo. Buck Clayton went into the wings with as much dignity as he could muster, after having proved that he can play well despite any odds.

Voilà! We swear we have been objective and have recounted barely half of the horrors to be heard that night.

Racism Lives: White vs. Black

by Michel Delaroche

(*Jazz News*: June, 1950)

Certain critics (far from the least important of them) have increasingly made it a practice (first in England and Australia, now in America) to launch frontal assaults against black music.

The phenomenon is nothing new.

Since 1920, white people in the music business have tried to profit from exploiting the racial prejudice which still exists in the United States. It is necessary only to cite the following examples: Paul Whiteman, who was crowned King of Jazz despite the existence of a certain Fletcher Henderson; Red Nichols, who cut more records than three King Olivers combined; Jimmy Dorsey (who has begun to record again); the Casa Loma Orchestra; Goldkette and Goodman . . . all of them have far busier schedules than black bands of equal or greater talent. For a more contemporary example, Dizzy Gillespie would certainly compete better against Stan Kenton if he turned his manificent big band into a Kentonesque noise machine.

All of which is no surprise. The general public is just as unenlightened. A similar syndrome is apparent in literature and the cinema – there are ten Fernandel movies for every *Devil in the Flesh*. All of this would not be worth talking about were it not for the fact that the phenomenon is growing. Matters are beginning to get out of hand and it is imperative to start doing something about it.

The journalists who promulgate the problem use one of three methods . . .

1) Honesty – (Roger Bell in issue no. 8 of the *Australian Jazz Quarterly*).

2) Hypocrisy – (Leonard Feather's recent 'Crow Jim' article).

3) Objectivity – a cynical method which is in fact no 'method' at all (see all the recent issues of *Down Beat*).

1) The Honest Method will, if nothing else, make you cringe. In fact this is the least dangerous method because in general it comes out of such obvious sectarianism, from such a narrow parochial spirit that it unmasks itself by definition.

The Honest Method led Roger Bell to write this absolutely incredible passage . . .

> It is perfectly clear that at the present time, black Americans have deserted jazz. The only coloured men who play worthwhile music play the same music they have played for years; they are obviously not prepared to create anything new in the idiom. They've had their time. While the young coloured musicians have turned in a mass to swing and bebop. The future of jazz, if it has one, is consequently currently entirely in the hands of young whites.

Understand that when he says 'swing' or 'bebop', Roger Bell is euphemistically referring to any jazz music more recent than approximately 1935. Jazz stopped in 1945 for certain critics, and it is already absolutely absurd to eliminate men like Parker, Dizzy, Miles Davis, Ernie Royal and Max Roach from the ranks, but Bell goes ten years further. The conclusion is unavoidable, since he employs the term 'Swing' in the American stylistic sense; he is eliminating Duke Ellington, Count Basie and Lionel

Hampton in one fell swoop.

He has defined the word 'jazz' in the most narrow terms. This said, if jazz is really how Bell defines it, he is absolutely correct in concluding that young blacks no longer want any part of it. Certainly none of them is tempted to play like Ward Pinkett or Papa Mutt Carey any more, and that's fine; I am far from saying that either Ward or Papa is a bad musician – both are perfectly valid within the context of their time.

Take painting for a comparison: a Vermeer has no artistic value whatsoever unless it is a real Vermeer painted in his time, and perfect fakes painted recently by a very talented Dutchman lose all their meaning (even though they are pleasant to look at) because they were copied and have no historic context whatsoever.

These details notwithstanding, I repeat that pronouncements like those of Roger Bell are much less dangerous than one might think, principally due to the naïve assumptions from which they stem – another example of which is expressed on another page of Bell's article.

I am obliged to cite the long passage in its entirety because I want to prove that I am not quoting out of context – it is all too easy to get anybody you want to say whatever you want them to say by clever editing . . .

Bell writes:

I am convinced that jazz will in the near future move on to new forms and will find new vitality as soon as it is assimilated in Australia, England, France and other countries which are free from the influence of its birthplace, America.

Perhaps one of the biggest problems has been the recent revival of the New Orleans style which – because of the number and nature of books and articles written on the subject, and the reissuing of so many records – has had a major inhibiting effect on young white musicians. Many of them are terrified by the idea of playing something which does not sound like Ladnier or early Armstrong. They are overwhelmed by Jelly Roll Morton, the Hot Five and Seven, by all the Orys, Bunks and Bessies – the critics have told them so often that these people are the only ones of any value that they have become too timid to try to play anything at all other

than a lamentable pastiche of black things past. They rarely, if
at all, listen to the rich body of work by white giants like
Sharkey Bonano, Bix, Teschemacher and Hackett, music
which they might more readily assimilate because it is racially
more organic. These people have been too often defined as a
watered-down commercial copy – what a misnomer! – and
young white musicians are advised that the New Orleans style
is the only real thing.

I will never forget one evening in the house of an English
jazz critic of international renown. Seated at the piano,
playing the blues, Graeme Bell tried out unusual chordal
inversions and inhabitual licks here and there. The critic
remained standing quietly with a sad look on his face for a
while, and then he said: 'Why don't you play a real blues,
Graeme?' Graeme looked up and said: 'I know what you
want,' and began to bang out those old tattered licks which
one hears on every black blues record. The critic was
enraptured. He smiled from head to toe: 'That's it, old man!
That's real jazz.' Well, in all objectivity, it's laughable.

I am astonished every time I realize that jazz can give birth
to such ridiculously narrow and rigid judgements. This music
is by definition the antithesis of anything reactionary. Yet
these backward-looking people would rather spread their
narrow judgements than help renew the music.

Yes, Roger Bell wrote all of that. And it is hard indeed to
believe that the revolutionary world of jazz has been permeated
by such reactionary judgementalists – because in fact Roger is
himself one of them and he in fact confirms my own, opposing,
point of view.

There are three elements to point out . . .

a) Evidence of racism (his first sentence, and the tirade in
favour of white masters).

b) Overwhelming naïveté: the idea that Graeme Bell was able
to invent something not at least based on inventions of black
musicians accused by Roger Bell of not playing jazz any more,
makes him incompetent to talk about jazz. As if we could forget
about Mozart, Beethoven, Haydn and Bach while creating new
classical music.

c) Total lack of consistency – his final sentence criticizes others for his own faults.

To recapitulate, Roger concludes that white people are the only ones capable of renewing jazz because he gives the music a definition which eliminates three-quarters of it. Well, at least it's honest – stupid but honest. Just like the stupid honesty with which the Australians go about exterminating their own indigenous people, and with which South African whites are blissfully going down the same road.

Let's move on to the second, much more dangerous, method.

2) Hypocritical Method . . . doubly hypocritical because of its very nature and the personality explaining it – none other than Leonard Feather, an Englishman who emigrated to the US. In general Feather does his job as a critic, he's an acceptable pianist, he has put together some good bands and composed several pleasing tunes ('Scram'). The problem lies with one of his articles, the title of which is 'Crow Jim' (as opposed to 'Jim Crow'.) Feather maintains that 'Crow Jim' is the, so to speak, reigning European jazz philosophy.

Let's analyse it . . .

We know that the various prejudices and persecutions which victimize blacks in the US are summed up by the term 'Jim Crow'. According to Feather, the inverse spirit currently dominates Europe, where the poor white musicians, victims of 'Crow Jim', are not given the appreciation they deserve.

Certain white French musicians have been known to say something similar. Maurice Moufflard once attacked Dizzy Gillespie in the presence of Vian and Diéval, maintaining that he, Moufflard, played better than Dizzy, who had never even set foot in a music conservatory. Sometimes you hear others say: 'Ah! All you need is black skin to make it in this business.' The extraordinary thing is that this sort of thing is *always* said by the worst jazz musicians imaginable.

Feather's article is stupid and revolting as well as insipid. The stupidity is so basic that it does not even merit detailed analysis. It's enough to give a few examples to disprove his reasoning – the hisses and boos which greeted Kenny Hagood and even poor Kay Davis (both black), who were not singing 'jazzy' enough for the French audience; the enthusiastic applause for a Swedish group and Claude Luter during a recent festival. Stupid, revolting.

156

It's one thing for an Englishman to protest because blacks are blindly accepted in Europe. But he should not do that in America. The context is different. He can say such a thing over there only when racial prejudice becomes a thing of the past. Which, alas, is not just around the corner. (Remember what happened when King Cole wanted to move into a house in a white neighbourhood.) Until then Vido Musso Ventura Candoli Rogers can wait until they play as well as Lester or Miles for their genius to be recognized – they have a lot to learn while they wait.

3) Objective Method . . . otherwise known as 'Cynical'. This is the method used by those who spend their time giving birth to articles praising Dixieland recordings by putrid bands from Los Angeles and elsewhere – Pete Daily, Firehouse Five, Turk Murphy, Bob Scobey, Lu Watters, etcetera etcetera. One might excuse this sort of exercise in the European provinces where they do not know any better but not in the birthplace of jazz. Just mentioning these people is to ratify them. This must be protested against. And here I come back to Roger Bell – if you like white Dixieland, we are already blessed with authentics like Bix, the Bob Crosby Bobcats and several others. Unhappily, all those who copy them now do so for the dollar. There is no longer a smidgeon of creativity. They are fake Vermeers.

To conclude . . .

What is the danger of all this? Every time a record company releases some derivative obscenity, it leaves less room for the young musicians – the real ones, the young *black* ones. On this subject, all of the critics, even the most opinionated, are in agreement. What difference does it make if Panassié likes to call them 'moderns', or if Delaunay refers to them as 'boppers'. The fact remains that Wardell Gray, who began by imitating Lester Young, is more important to jazz than the fossilized insincere Jimmy Dorsey. Just as Louis Armstrong, who began by imitating King Oliver, created his own page in jazz history. I'm not trying to say that Wardell Gray is as important as Louis Armstrong – you could call him Joe Smith or Pierre Dupont, it wouldn't matter.

It is simply more of a sure thing to bet on a representative of this black race which created jazz, the only race – since the decline of the yellow and the white – which still has a chance to breathe fresh, new, uninhibited, revolutionary life into the world of the arts. Revolutionary like, in fact, jazz was in its infancy, like it still is when played by blacks, these blacks who have made it, who still make it and will continue to make it something unique . . . unless, that is, they are stabbled in the back by the Feathers.

CHARLIE SHAVERS

(*Jazz Hot*: March, 1953)

Charlie James Shavers was born in New York on 3 August, 1917 – the same year as King Cole – and he began by playing the banjo before teaching himself trumpet, according to the *Esquire Jazz Book*. He made his professional debut in 1935. In 1936, he played with the Blue Ribbon Band, then John Kirby (1937–43) and recorded with dozens of others. For a while he led his own quintet, which recorded several sides for Vogue which had short lives in America.

Five years younger than Roy Eldridge, he's the same age as Dizzy (1917 was a banner year for the trumpet). Shavers's style developed between 1935–45. It can be inferred from this that he was influenced more by Roy and Rex Stewart than by Louis – we infer it with the certitude of retrospect. If we had had to predict it, my dear, we would have been a lot less clever. In short, Shavers has his own style. And yet he's hardly known in France. All the more reason to talk about him; better late than not at all.

Hardly known. What a shame. Because he's much better than what we've heard of his playing with Bechet on 'I'm Comin' Virginia' and 'Georgia Cabin'. Well now, these two sides are a good point of departure. I don't have them here at the moment, but I remember that Shavers seemed to parody Bechet. Was it on purpose? Or was he overcome by the influence of the old master? In short, he imitated the speed and expressiveness of the soprano saxophone. Which by itself reveals two talents: technique and suppleness. And perhaps one fault: is he too susceptible to the influence of others? Does he lack personality?

When you mention Shavers to musicians who know him, they unanimously compliment his incredible technique. That's a fact. However he's not considered 'hip', there's no school following him as with Louis, Roy, Dizzy, Miles. This confirms the same lack of personality that keeps Jonah Jones out of the top echelon.

Fine. But if he's prone to the influence of others, it proves that he at least knows how to listen to the people he plays with. He has ears. Let's go on from there.

'Laguna Leap' (with Herbie Haymer). What's this? A fearlessly 'bopesque' unison line? A solo containing all the stylistic elements we've heard from Dizzy? That's weird! This guy is capable of playing like either Bechet or Dizzy.

Ah ha! Shavers, Charlie. You are a professional musician. OK, OK, don't worry, we'll get to the bottom of you yet. You're just doing your job. You don't care about the rest. That's why you play like this one or that one. Imitating styles can be a style in itself. You have a sense of humour – not to be laughed at – *good* humour with nuance and Pataphysique.*

But then you fly off to the other extreme on 'Black Market Stuff'. What is this sudden grandiloquence? A big brilliant sound, enormous breadth? This, Shavers, is the *real* you.

To continue, you are more emotional than intellectual. You prefer rum to cognac, meat and fruit to vegetables and cake, and to make it spicier I'll even go so far as to say that you like rice more than spaghetti, or anyway overcooked spaghetti.

You'll play whatever they play because their style is important to them. But as I said, you cut two sides under your own name, those two Vogue records, and they are made of transparent plastic covered with terribly ugly drawings. Under your own name, so you must be responsible for that.

Translator's note: Vian, Raymond Queneau and others created the College of Pataphysics. It was Dadaist, absurd. They were serious about not taking themselves seriously.

'Serenade to a Pair of Nylons'. Your portrait is on the jacket – happy smile, apple-cheeked, generous nose and lips, large flat ears. Your own quintet, Shavers.

Here's one with Buddy DeFranco. You play the melody and a short solo muted. An authoritative, wide vibrato. Buddy doesn't play too bad, not really. I don't exactly detest him. And the rhythm section, very 4/4, is light and swinging. Allegro return of Shavers disguised as a Spaniard. Fanfare. Henry Allen could learn something here. But you're sweating, Shavers, almost biting your mouthpiece off. That calls to mind the word 'lyrical'.

Shavers, either I'm making a big mistake or you're definitely not homosexual. And unless I'm making an even bigger mistake, you're not faithful to your chick either.

'Broadjump', on the other side, kicks off at a breakneck tempo. But don't push too hard, Shavers, you'll never be a bopper (neither would Dizzy if he hadn't married an intellectual). You're definitely pre-war. You were twenty in 1937. But what a beautiful sound, what a clean attack, what lovely technique! And articulation better than just good – a bit frenetic, perhaps, and the lines do not flow very well. In step with Jonah Jones. So what about your coda? Rex Stewart did that too . . . a triple-tongued staccato, I believe, Shavers. Either it was a mistake, or else you're laughing again. Can't you be serious for three minutes?

'If I Had You'. That's a very pretty song, Shavers. Can you see it, it's like a colour cover of *True Romance*. You're sentimental, Shavers. A tender inflection right there, yes – just like Lawrence Brown. Ha! A sentimental tempo isn't so bad if you play it with heart and 'soul'.

Deep down, Shavers, didn't it bore you to play with Bechet? Buddy does nice things as usual. You take the tune out muted. Vehemence. A cracked note. Rex is your man. A beautiful clear, flamboyant ending.

'Musicomania', the flip side. Your pianist has a Basieite touch, he's not bad. John Potaker? Never heard of him. Alvin Stoller on drums, clean and efficient. Sidney Block on bass. Straight-ahead, Shavers, beautiful. That tasty arpeggio – do, mi, sol, do, mi, sol, do – it's strong. And such hard tonguing, not everyone can do that. No, that's also your style – making it sound easy.

Shavers, your case is clear. You play very well, but you also have more passion for life than for music. Which is to say in other words that you love all music, not just your little horn. People probably tell you sometimes that you lack taste, Charlie. Some undernourished intellectual will certainly reproach you for it. But Balzac too, you know ... Absence of taste, when combined with enough confidence, becomes a style in itself. You could have gone further. You were born just a little too early – you didn't hear what you should have heard when you could have heard it. What about your education? After all, it must not have been easy to become Shavers. It says born such and such a date, 1917 – but born under what circumstances? Suffering is often not in the official biography. Personally, Shavers, I'm one of your fans. You let the fire take hold of you – but not all the time because it's so nice outside that it seems dumb to slave away while it's so much fun to hang out in the park or the bars. With a good guru, you might have been a bigger Shavers. With Duke, for example.

Goodbye, Shavers. I'm going to hear you with Jazz at the Philharmonic and you'll probably play with so much humour you'll make yourself laugh. While I might be embarrassed – well, not too embarrassed because you're really a nice guy.

HALF A CENTURY OF JAZZ (1)

(*La Parisienne*: February, 1953)

It's terribly difficult to write intelligently about jazz, as the following article will prove.

Everybody has their own definition of the word. I feel like asking my editor here at *La Parisienne*: 'Can't I write an article about spiders? Coal dust? Mustard?' But I know what the answer would be so, OK, let's try and harness the beast. What a diabolical task – to talk about what you love in plain, simple, direct language.

I could recommend that the reader go out and buy one of the many books on the subject. It's becoming an impressively long list. Big, little, hardbound, soft-cover books – out-of-print books, books a-go-go. Plus all those articles in all those magazines. In every language, including Japanese. That's right, there are Hot Clubs in Tokyo, India, Australia and South America. Maybe even behind the iron curtain, who knows?

But I refuse to assume responsibility for all those books. I will not recommend them to the reader. And magazines minister only to people who do not have the patience to read books, good or bad, while dictionaries are for those who don't want to read anything at all. We wouldn't want our nice neat little reader to get a long-playing king-size migraine. He'd finish by curling up with the adventures of Camembert-Bidet for a modicum of spiritual peace after reading so many contradictory opinions. Take the following example: 'As a trained biologist, I look on jazz as a living being which must be studied from conception through infancy, maturity and old age' (Bernard Heuvelmans, *From Bamboula to Bebop*).

The reader will immediately conclude from the above that jazz is on its last legs, that it is a senior citizen, and he'll hit the ceiling later when he reads, in the book I am preparing on the subject, that this is not true at all, that the musicians who continue to create and enrich this lively art form are not at all ready to let it grow senile before they have even had a chance to give birth to their own licks. But I can see in your eyes the lewd blue-eyed sparkle reflecting the analytical Cartesian beast which inhabits the soul of every Frenchman: 'You'd better get down to defining "jazz", old man. You're only playing word games, and that just isn't done in this country.'

Weak-kneed and on the defensive, I can only respond that there are words which oblige you to play games. Nothing else will do. Jazz is one of them. As Bernard Heuvelmans is a nice man, I will not follow the thread of the vituperous attack which I began above. But I return to his own definition, while pointing out that he is playing word games of his own: 'Whatever the context of the specific material in question, jazz is essentially black American music' (op cit).

To which we comment . . .

– As Heuvelmans himself recalls, the first blacks came to Louisiana, the 'birthplace of jazz', in about 1712.

– Due to the confluence of so many diverse factors, some interesting flavours emerged from the Afro-American bouquet.

– Even more diverse factors continued to influence this Whatchamacallit.

– So there is no reason to conclude that 'this good old music is jazz and that terrible new stuff ain't'. Because the process is far from finished. Obviously it would make certain people very happy if it were.

– On the other hand it is not easy for some Americans to feel obliged to respect black people for their 'diga-diga-doo', the only artistic competition these Statesiders can drum up against our venerable European traditions.

– I am now going to escape astutely from the corner I have painted myself into by a valiant sortee to the root of the problem.

My friend Eddie has a black mahogany television set. The other day, watching a documentary about African music at his house, I thought about jazz each time I saw one of those remarkable collective dance numbers which are de rigueur for this sort of film. There were admirable polyrhythmic moments – I'll never forget a sequence where the natives were preceded by (that is to say followed by, they were moving forward backwards) tambours and marimbas. But watching and listening to this film, which seemed to be an honest effort, made me want to shout out still one more time my disagreement with those who claim that rhythm is the dominant element in African music.

Perhaps it is dominant for the claimers in question, but it is also possible that they mistake notes for noise. Personally, I find this music perfectly balanced – polymelody is just as important as polyrhythm. The melodies which come out of these ancient wooden instruments are perhaps even more complex than those played on a Pleyel quadruple-grand piano, just as agreeable and, to my taste, often more contemporary. I love to hear all those notes together, even when they chafe a bit.

Africans who emigrated to the States – let it be said, rather unwillingly – before they were United, brought their music with them and it thrived there. Co-opted little by little by the whites, the black music assimilated eccentric elements such as Protestant hymns, French quadrilles, marches, polkas and even the sound of Babcock and Wilcox heaters which were soon discarded when it was found that they served no useful purpose.

The Africans were introduced to European instruments. Not content with the traditional limitations of those instruments, they took great pleasure in demolishing the old rules concerning the defined 'expressive' qualities of winds and strings. They played for parties and picnics, learned to read music, worked with white musicians, developed the blues which, we should point out, was born long before they reached New Orleans, drank strong whisky, led parades for funerals and weddings and learned little by little how to talk to the growing multitude of idiots who began to write about all of these things.

It's bizarre – critics all agree about one point. They trace jazz back to a birthdate around the year 1900. They also all worship the great trumpet player Buddy Bolden, who was committed to an insane asylum in 1907 and died in 1931. Yet not one of us ever heard him.

I would love to paint a lovely portrait of the Storyville brothels and the Creole beauties in Lulu White's establishment; it would be like painting the Sistene Chapel of the time. I would like to evoke the captivating nights of New Orleans with the accents of the emerging sound of jazz murmuring like a contented baby in its cradle. But that would be as stupid for you to read as for me to write.

There are, after all, more important things to say about jazz. Now that we both agree it exists, let's try and avoid injecting metaphysical problems into something that is flourishing quite well without us. The 'How' of it appears to be more interesting to deal with than the 'What'.

So go back to 1917, the year the navy closed the red-light district of New Orleans after a brawl of riotous proportions. Thus deprived of work, the musicians went up the Mississippi River and planted their little jazz onions everywhere. They grew and flourished everywhere. This version of the story makes me giggle, not to say fall down laughing. It seems to me that progress in recording technique and sound reproduction are much more important. Taking the risk of excommunication, I dare say that Pathé-Marconi played a more important role than the closing of the whorehouses in Storyville.

Ragtime, one of the earliest forms of jazz, developed with vigour at the beginning of the century and conquered the world. The piano music called ragtime benefited from the player piano (with perforated rolls) and then its notation on paper. So, even admitting that the closing of the brothels of Storyville (which I deplore as much as any other reasonable man) played a role in the history of jazz, I hold that recording, and later the radio, are the real travelling salesmen to whom we owe our daily jazz, in whatever form we prefer.

Grosso modo, from 1917, with the first recordings, we can begin to regard jazz from an historical point of view. Every jazz fan knows that in 1919 the Swiss orchestra conductor Ernest Ansermet discovered this thing we're talking about when he listened to a black band and jazz was the subject of his now famous article in the *Revue Romand*. Everybody also knows that Sidney Bechet played in the band in question, the Southern Syncopated Orchestra. And if everybody didn't know it, they do now.

Now I am forced to divide this history into periods – from 1920 to 1935, 1935 to 1940, etcetera. But it's so out of place and corny – if nothing else, you see, I'm honest. There's no rhyme nor reason to it. It's obviously impossible to judge and analyse certain records from the past only from memory. And if I play them again, now, me, a 1953 Vian who already heard them in 1935, how can I have the objectivity to arrive at a judgement relevant to their own time? I've always asked myself how one of my contemporaries can dare write a book about Balzac. I answer myself – because that's the way the literary game is played. You see, I am a very intellectual jazz critic.

Actually, to tell the truth, I'm always just itching to step out on a limb and saw myself off. Which is of no importance whatsoever, except to introduce the following observation. When you push a jazz fan (your moderately intelligent fanatic fan) up against the wall, all he can come up with by way of analysis is names names names. Armstrong, Fletcher, Duke, Fats, Parker etcetera. OK, we could surely group them into stylistic boxes with accompanying pontifical decisive arguments (it's not too hard to win any argument if you are decisive enough) to prove we are right. But what purpose does it serve, this mania to mummify everything?

At the age of twenty, today's French writers have nothing more pressing to do than publish the first volume of their memoirs. At thirty (if they have become famous), they write volume two. This is called 'discovering the man behind the novelist'. But he has never been lost, the man, he's always there. It's the novel which is lost. We'll write your biography in a bright contemporary style, but this is only 'the first day of the rest of your life', as the Americans like to say. No?

We lean too much on history in France. Does that mean we are unhappy? Happy people do not dwell on past history. The past of jazz should not be dwelt on. Jazz is not sad, it is living music, it is swarming and bustling with life! It is only fifty years old. Fifty! Imagine! They are already trying to bury it.

Heuvelmans is trying to pass senility under our noses like a sick man's bedpan. We'd better laugh and run for our lives. It's not yet time to go and hide in numbered bank vaults.

And it is time to say, reader, my dear friend, reader, buy or steal 500 Duke Ellington records and you are sure to end up with at least 450 great jazz records. Forget the explainers, because *nihil est in comentario quod non primum fuerit in operibus.* Don't give me that funny look, I'm just proving how literate I am.

Now let us kneel and listen together.

HALF A CENTURY OF JAZZ (2)

(*La Parisienne*: February, 1953)

Jazz is fifty years old. Fifty years plus radio play and record distribution equals a lot more than that in cosmic time – taking into account the increased diffusion and its consequent impact.

In this short period, more masterful jazz musicians have been born than great masters of so-called 'serious' music in 300 years. Although this is true enough, you should remember that jazz critics, simple souls that they are, have a dire need to discover geniuses. Supercritic Hugues Panassié makes himself look silly ten times a year by exclaiming ten times a year – 'Soandso is without doubt the greatest.' Soandso, I wish to make clear, is somebody else each time. Genius is the currency of jazz criticism (in all criticism, as a matter of fact, but let's not trespass). Critics feed off genius; discovering it proves their competence. They find it in performance after performance, on every stage. And we continue to read over and over that 'Louis Armstrong is jazz personified. He'll blow you through the roof.' In 100 years we'll have a lot more than double the geniuses we have now. I'll be glad to prove it to you. Let's make an appointment; mark your calendar.

The last thing I want to do is to refer you to all those idiotic jazz magazines in which you read the same stupidity ten times in ten different places. It's true, you know, believe me, we all copy from each other.*

Happily, jazz is music. And music has an essential charactistic which is rather neglected in this day and age. You *listen* to it, that's its charm. So after you've digested the effusive outpourings of miscellaneous thirteenth-hour enthusiasts, you still have the albums, the records inside them and your record player. Geniuses evaporate once the needle hits the wax. Very few remain. Normality returns – we forget about epochs, and 'ruptures with the past'. We come back to the essence, the perfect continuity of all things. Everything in jazz is a result of what went before and, listening, we are reassured that all is well. We are always in a primitive era and while it may be commodious and amusing to make chapters and sub-chapters, the only real classification which makes any sense is alphabetical.

Jazz is still being born. One proof is the fact that it never stays the same for very long. For example, take the little event which has caused the flowing of the most critink since the Liberation – the bebop affair. The recordings of Charlie Parker and Dizzy Gillespie caused an outcry of indignation when they were released in France – people screamed that they were totally rejecting the past, profoundly modifying the very roots of jazz – distorting the rhythmic structure, mutilating the melodies, fooling around shamefully with harmony, abusing the flatted fifth, the augmented fourth, these infuriating young prometheans with the maddening tendency to use 11th chords, 13th chords, 75th chords and on and on. Critics got together, listened once or twice and then proceeded to tear it all apart toute de suite. The very same critics who admit quite readily that their very own tame little jazz was formerly nourished by important presenters of Western repertoire like the Mormon Tabernacle Choir of Oshkosh now scream bloody murder when Gillespie adds a bongo player to his big band. Just think! A Cuban who was not born in New Orleans!

It's really bizarre. Now that poor jazz has for once managed to

---

*It's like grafting from one plant to another. Or like in elementary-school maths, when I copy my homework from Dupont who copied it from Margerie . . . which one of us succeeds in life?

incorporate some of its original African influences, these critics tear out its feathers, cause a 'schism' in the heart of the Hot Clubs and go to fight the lions in the arena. While jazz continues to do quite well without them, thank you very much. 'Bop is the walking death!' screams one. 'Vive le bop!' the other shouts back. And each of them believes he has won his case.

As copy, furnishing material for articles, bop is no longer a current event.* However, in reality, it has inserted itself exactly in its proper chronological place (curious, it seems to me that La Palisse† himself would not deny having said this. Am I wrong?) An uncountable number of people have been influenced by bop records – which in fact are not 'revolutionary' at all, original as they may be – released since 1940 by the Minton's crowd: Gillespie, Parker, Clarke, Monk and their disciples. It would be possible, with the greatest of ease, to count each link of the chain that ties a traditionalist like Sidney Bechet, taking into account all the same pop songs they have used, to an 'avant gardist' like Parker, whose favourite musician, I am told, is Paul Hindemith. This, however, should, any historical influence notwithstanding, be enough to prove that these two gentlemen do not play the same style of music a-tall.

Critics have small ears. If they were bigger, they would be able to understand that, oh unmitigated blessing, we are every one of us bathing in the same delicious chaos. All of this comes and goes and agitates and organizes itself without need for words, and musicians follow their own simple little paths waving their own personal black flags.

One of them above all: Mr Ellington. Excuse me. Lord Ellington.

Because I am by nature affectionate and hospitable, I often invite friends to my place so that I can beat their brains out with my records. Very odd – no matter what their taste, they all

---

*'Event' almost rhymes with elephant, so I'll leave it instead of substituting the more economical 'news' – it's not easy to come up with something that rhymes with elephant.
†*Translator's note*: the hero of a nineteenth-century song who was always pronouncing pompous redudancies.

eventually ask to hear the same ones. Ellington records. He's got it *all* – if not always all, at least always all in an embryonic stage.

It goes without saying that Ellington is not the only musician to have made excellent jazz records. He has, however, to my knowledge, made more of them than anyone else. He is the only one prodigious and prolific enough to dwarf even Armstrong. Because Duke's instrument is an entire fifteen-piece orchestra. To compare his creative power, perpetual self-renewal and will to take risks to Picasso does not overestimate either one of them.

So as it turns out we have our geniuses whether we like it or not.* Ellington has dominated jazz music ever since it was first recorded. He is its past and future at the same time. His personality has indelibly marked several generations of instrumentalists and arrangers. He was there almost at the beginning – his first recordings date from around 1925. Voilà! Here is somebody who hasn't finished, who keeps going, who keeps going very well indeed, thank you very much (again). What does he have to do with senility? Paragraphs? Ruptures? Schisms? What does he have to do with irrelevances like Stan Kenton, for example? In 1936, Kenton recorded 'Reminiscing in Tempo', which, its faults apart, was much more audacious at the time than all his diverse 'Artistrys' in This or That in 1953. I cite Kenton because he is one famous bandleader whom, actively encouraged by Mr Kenton himself, people call 'progressive'. Though I can think of nothing more appalling than the poverty of imagination of his arrangements for his polka band in heat.†

But we stray too far afield from Ellingtonian pastures. Instead, let's prepare to hit the ground running with an answer to the following insidious question with which some of you out there are preparing to shoot me down:

'You miserable rodent, tell us how are we supposed to know what's real jazz and what isn't?'

This question is always enormously embarrassing for critics. The Americans get themselves out of the fix with an astute answer. They have the luck to be able to claim that 'American popular music' is all in 4/4 time, just like jazz, and they put it all

---

*In this case, it also serves my purpose to say so.
†No, 'in heat' is not a new dance I invented.

in the same bag under the same name,* mixing the rags with the napkins. And we others, barbaric Zeuropeans, are we stuck with our waltzes and bal musettes? But let's go further. Can we really baptize everything in 4/4 'jazz'? You need criteria, criteria, damn it! We have been labouring over this problem for a long time in France, and it's going to go on a lot longer, like Fermat's theories.† The rest of the world is well aware of it – oh how we Cartesians labour to define that subtle and mysterious thing, swing. Many definitions have been given to this holy word. We have carped a lot about the brand of swing specific to black music, which whites, with the help of some miracles and by the grace of God, can sometimes copy under certain circumstances. Oh, yeah, it sure would be nice to dispose of this sort of phlogiston. It would simplify everything and we would know where we are going. But, voilà, we have no idea where we're going, which is one good illustration of the bankruptcy of criticism in general. Where some find swing, others hear nothing but slick technique, and the humour of some of Lunceford's languorous presentations, the very soul of swing for the former, totally escapes the latter who consider them nothing more than wet marshmallows.

The truth, I believe, is both simple and deceiving, like a naked woman. When a classical musician interprets one page of Bach he must be impregnated with the relevant tradition. A jazz musician will not play real jazz unless he respects his own tradition: black tradition, black American tradition. And here we come to the root of the problem. A minority which, like all oppressed minorities, guards its secrets, does not want to reveal them to the first majoritarian who comes along. So an initiation period is necessary. This is obviously no problem for a young black musician who swims in the culture, but a white player will have to spend most of his learning period getting rid of his own tradition.

Let us continue to try and come to terms with the puzzling question of swing. It is also true that the black tradition in question is not yet rigid and is enriched with new elements from

---

*I said their answer was 'astute', but come to think of it it's pretty dumb.
†*Translator's note*: a seventeenth-century mathematician who published one theory after another often without taking the time to prove them.

day to day, like the Cuban influence mentioned above. Go ahead then, try to analyse an art which changes daily! And isn't the best illustration of this thesis the recent 'revival', as they say, of the New Orleans style, a revival – thanks to the International Union of Unimaginative Youths – of the tunes and improvisations of King Oliver, Johnny Dodds, Jimmie Noone . . . in short all the great names from the twenties? Almost all of them are dead, and their records are frozen in that old style. Rich white boys, with such stable points of reference, have to do no more than re-create exact replicas with a fairly close approximation of the ambience of the period. But just when critics and musicians begin to understand this one moment in the life of jazz, it grows new wings, flies a little further and everything begins one more time. You need subtle and expandable ears to follow it, because the hustle and bustle of jazz is the image of the hustling and bustling of fifteen million blacks who, persecuted and terrorized, are trying to make their place in the 'Etazunis'* through their tears and hard work.

Jazz criticism is further confused by a serious problem: the ephemeral nature of the audience. In reality, white people are interested in jazz only in their adolescent years. They get carried away listening to the first smooth talker who comes along, about whom more opinions are expressed than in an economists' convention. And suddenly it's all over. They get married and no longer have the time or the energy to go on listening. Jazz does not interest them any longer because it is not sentimental music. Worse, it is difficult to find good jazz to listen to. It's not exactly on every street corner, and when the radio grinds you down all year long with the same old Piaffites and Chevalieresques one after the other, you get tired fast. You need passion for jazz and, alas, we do not remain young at heart for long chez nous.

Yes, indeed, the public renews itself quickly. I am reminded of a comic book I read around 1933, in which I particularly liked one of the strips. Many years later I stumbled on another issue of the same comic by chance. It was ten years older – or younger; in short, 1923. It had exactly the same story-board. And the editors knew their business. At their readers' age, ten

---

Translator's note: word play on 'Etats-Unis' (United States in French) and 'Nazis'.

years equals a generation. The young audience, including the audience for jazz, is renewed with terrifying speed. But should this cause us to remain with the same premises for ever, spend our entire life in a playground? Certain critics are quite happy to do just that. I am not saying that anybody over twenty-five is unable to understand or love jazz, but rare are those who can maintain their passion at a high enough level to continue the sacrifices the serious fan is forced to make. This reactor works only at a high temperature; it absorbs a lot of warmth.

Jazz criticism is not maturing (as though any critic ever matures). It confines itself to a very small territory. It turns in circles, reimposes the same rudiments, it analyses, stammers and dissects dead platters. It does not go any further than this sort of thing .. 'Mr Soandso believes that Mr Soandso is a better musician than Mr Soandso. But Mr Soandso is a cad because the truth of the matter is that Mr Soandso is actually the best.' That about sums it up. There are other sorts of maniacs, those who say: 'Jazz is this and not anything else and people who say that is jazz are idiots because jazz, I tell you, is *this*.' Thus, for example, speaks Mezzrow. The Papacy has its converts.

On the other hand, to conclude, there are those who are in no hurry to crown or classify – those who mock accepted values, who rejoice when the unexpected wipes out their theories, who write articles on jazz because it's fun, who are interested in it because it's music. When these people put records on their turntables and play them, they quickly understand that a good number of jazz records hold their own against Albinoni, Berg and Ravel. And it amuses them to read other people's articles about their favourite sport because they are pleased when it is spoken about at all, even by idiots (idiots can be fun).

These good people, I fondly hope, are my readers. I love people who know how to laugh, even if they laugh at me.

INDEX